ℋEALTHY STRING PLAYING

PHYSICAL WELLNESS TIPS FROM THE PAGES OF *Strings* MAGAZINE

T0066129

ISBN-13: 978-1-423-41808-5
ISBN-10: 1-423-41808-5

Visit Hal Leonard Online at
www.halleonard.com

In Australia Contact:
Hal Leonard Australia Pty. Ltd.
4 Lentara Court
Cheltenham, Victoria, 3192 Australia
Email: ausadmin@halleonard.com

STRING LETTER PUBLISHING

EXCLUSIVELY DISTRIBUTED BY

HAL•LEONARD®
CORPORATION

7777 W. BLUEMOUND RD. P.O. BOX 13819 MILWAUKEE, WI 53213

Contents

Introduction

Among musicians, string players account for the highest percentage of both chronic and acute performance-related injuries. *Healthy String Playing* provides a concise resource for string musicians, presenting in-depth information on treatment, prevention, and wellness.

Taken from the pages of *Strings* magazine, the articles collected here address critical issues such as repetitive stress injury, performance anxiety, playing hurt, and treatment options. Chapters on exercise, stretching, Pilates, yoga, and other wellness topics offer suggestions on how to stay in top playing form.

Personal stories from working musicians whose lives have been touched by music-related injuries, and information from leading performance-medicine professionals will help you identify and address potential injury-producing habits. Here the myth of "no pain, no gain" is soundly dismissed. Our contributors believe that playing a stringed instrument can and should be done comfortably and vitally for a lifetime. Play on!

Today, the most pressing need for enlightened care, and for future research, involves those unique and unusual elements of playing that take a specific toll on the body.

-Joan Hamilton

The Healthy String Player

1

By Joan Hamilton

AT SOME HOSPITALS these days, it's difficult to tell whether doctors are conducting examinations or recitals. "People are singing in my office all the time," says Robert Sataloff, a Philadelphia otolaryngologist. "I've got a nice big room where patients can bring their instruments and play," says Chicago internist Alice Brandfonbrener.

A new technique to soothe the savage virus? An antidote to waiting-room muzak? Hardly. Sataloff, Brandfonbrener, and others who practice a burgeoning sub-specialty called "performance medicine" are simply plying their trade.

The medical maladies of musicians are varied and complex. String players in particular can suffer troubles that range from untamable stage fright, creating bow tremors, to permanent nerve damage resulting from inflamed joints. Yet competitive pressures, exhausting travel schedules, and plain fear often mean years of delay before players seek help for a persistent pain. Even when they do break down and make an appointment, believes Sataloff, director of the Arts Medicine Center at Thomas Jefferson University Hospital, too often they confront a medical community "deficient in experience and expertise."

Because many doctors don't understand what a dramatic difference a seemingly small pain can make in performance, they sometimes tell musicians they are hypochondriacs. Or they suggest psychiatric help, suspecting the mind is manufacturing pain at the mere touch of the instrument. Or worse, players are "told to just stop playing until the problem is solved, by doctors who don't realize that music is an integral part of these people," says Dr. David Rosenthal, director of the Medical Center for the Performing Arts at Norristown, Pennsylvania's Suburban General Hospital. The result: frustration, and sometimes irreparable physical damage.

A handful of doctors, and a few courageous performers who've come forward to admit that their pleasure can also be their pain, are beginning to change this climate. Many large cities—including New York, Chicago, San Francisco, Los Angeles, Denver, Philadelphia, and Cleveland—now have major hospitals with resources specifically directed to the treatment of performing artists. Many of the physicians and therapists in these centers are musicians, singers, or dancers themselves. They are better able to understand the causes and treatments for these injuries, as well as the passions and pressures of players.

Growth in the specialty comes none too soon. According to a recent survey spearheaded by the International Conference of Symphony & Opera Musicians (ICSOM), fully seventy-six percent of the reporting membership tell of at least one medical problem they consider severe in terms of its effect on their performance. String players are hit hardest: eighty-four percent report at least one problem; seventy-eight percent indicate the problem is severe. The most common musculo-skeletal problems are of the neck, back, shoulders, hands, and elbows, while the most common discomforts overall are eye strain and stage fright.

These statistics don't surprise Dr. Brandfonbrener. Several years ago Brandfonbrener, who is not a musician but whose four children all play stringed instruments, grew increasingly concerned about injuries she saw among young players. About the same time, Gary Graffman, noted pianist and former director of the Curtis Institute of Music, came forward to discuss a debilitating condition in his hands that was curtailing his ability to play. Gradually specialists in various medical centers began to compare notes. Brandfonbrener is now one of the nation's leading authorities on the subject, and edits the *Medical Problems of Performing Artists* journal. Two years ago she set up her specialized practice at Northwestern Memorial Hospital in Chicago, and now sees more than seventy patients per month. "It's been humbling. We wish we knew a lot more than we do," she says. "What we do know is that historically, musicians have not gotten good care."

Turning that situation around is neither an easy nor a quick task. On the one hand, the changing health-care climate and increased competition among doctors is pushing many into joining specialized practices. But now that a number of clinics are in place, Brandfonbrener and other specialists say that education is the key to improving the health of musicians. Once they begin to realize that they can find not just a sympathetic medical ear, but that they can in fact be helped, musicians are lining up. "Symphony musicians had basically been in the closet with hand, mouth, and other injuries. Nobody wanted to talk about conditions related to medical disability," says Melanie Burrell, a cellist with the Denver Symphony and chairperson of ICSOM. "Now there is tremendous interest in these new clinics." Notes Brandfonbrener, "When we ask about specific techniques and positions, we see their eyes light up: 'Ah, somebody who understands!' "

A violinist with a major California orchestra recalls the origins of her performance-related injury—the pain and frustrations accompanying her attempt at a promotion. "I needed to practice more difficult pieces and undergo an audition," she recalls, so even when tingling and numbness began in her left hand, she kept to her rigorous workouts. Because of the persistent pain and weakness, she eventually failed her audition. Finally, she sought the help of Dr. Michael Charness, a physician with the University of California at San Francisco Performance Medicine Clinic, and a pianist who had suffered a similar injury himself. He recommended rest and eventually surgery. Today she is back in top shape. "Dr. Charness understood how frustrated I felt about not being able to play because he, himself, had had an injury," she says.

Such stories are becoming more common. In New York, a state grant allows a group from the New York State Health & Safety Program to give occupational health workshops to music organizations. The first conference devoted to the subject organized by an orchestra took place in Minnesota. And Brandfonbrener and other specialists say they are getting more requests to speak than they can fill.

Yet specialists complain that dollars to promote education about music medicine are still relatively scarce. Unlike the explosion of sports medicine in the 1970s, which was led by concerned professional sports teams trying to protect their players, "We do not have major financial backing," says Brandfonbrener. "I don't know why it's not a bigger issue in union contracts and in collective bargaining. There should be more room for preventive medicine. Symphonies go through two hundred to three hundred people to choose a player. Why don't we regard them like we do [former Chicago Bears quarterback Jim] McMahon?"

To most symphony musicians, the answer is all too obvious. "Itzhak Perlman can make demands. Anyone else can be replaced in an instant," says the New York project's director, Miriam Daum. Agrees Burrell, "We do not have stars like the teams do. We don't have doctors traveling with us." But expectations nonetheless run high: "There is tremendous pressure for us to create magic, to look like a ballet where everything seems flawless and effortless." And while the star athlete is paid well to perform at top levels for a relatively few years, most musicians face a lifetime of practice and competition.

Musicians also come in many sizes, shapes, and situations. While a high-profile soloist may be able to demand concessions designed to protect his or her health, the traveling young professional trying to make ends meet may not even be able to afford health insurance. And for musicians, it is not the kind of dramatic, acute injury that sidelines professional athletes that is most threatening. It's the years of playing with subtle pain and discomfort that do the damage. Often, musicians fall prey to the seemingly simple physical principal that if you bend and flex something enough times, it begins to wear out. Doctors call it "overuse."

Some mistakenly believe that overuse injuries are always the result of improper technique or posture. Improper technique can cause unnecessary stresses and strains, but more often it is "a sudden change of practice regimen," that signals the onset of pain, notes Phyllis Lehrer, head of the piano department at Westminster Choir College and an active member of the International Society for the Study of Tension and Performance. And very often that change comes about when the student makes his or her first big commitment to music. "A large number of injuries can be traced to the stresses of the conservatory," notes Daum.

Probably the bulk of the problem is self-inflicted, as students anxious to master their instruments devote countless hours to intense, repetitive practice. But some of that pressure is external, too. "The conservatory can be a wicked place," says Brandfonbrener. "Old-school faculty members preach, 'Keep practicing no matter how much it hurts. We went through it and so will you.' They've got to realize there's a limit to what your tissues will tolerate." Brandfonbrener, Lehrer, and others say they are trying to reach teachers to emphasize the importance of catching problems and pains before they lead to serious injuries. Lehrer for one puts a high priority on "helping students develop a technique that allows them to play with ease and intensity." She also holds workshops for teachers. "We'd like to work more closely with the medical community to share the ways people can work out their injuries. Often students get so demoralized and depressed," she says.

Indeed, many of the physicians who embrace performance medicine say that while they are pleased to help players overcome physical aches, they are just as concerned with emotional health and outlook. As musicians themselves, they are personally disturbed by the burnout and pain they see. Psychiatrist Peter Ostwald, director of the UCSF clinic, is also a violinist. He believes, "We shouldn't always be thinking of pathology. Why does the professional musician lose the love and joy of playing music? Amateurs, even the ones I treat, still seem to have it, yet so many professionals lose the love." If Ostwald and others like him have their way, in the future the answer is less likely to involve the nagging discomforts many players have come to accept—and hide.

What goes wrong?

"As doctors, we're not trained to understand the last five or ten percent of the body's physical capabilities," says Robert Sataloff, professional singer and music medicine specialist. "For a violinist or pianist, that's the five percent that makes the difference. The abnormalities are so much more subtle in a professional musician or singer that an observational and language barrier exists. If a singer says, 'Something's wrong with my throat, my high notes are gone,' he's still going to sound fine to a doctor used to listening to people dying of throat cancer."

That's why most of the new practitioners of performing arts medicine believe it's so important for doctors to be either musicians themselves, or intimately familiar with the typical life of a professional musician. "Musicians are really obsessive, compulsive people. The competition is not up front and often involves arbitrary standards. They carry around big loads of totally inappropriate guilt," observes Brandfonbrener. And that leads to a complex interplay of both physical and psychological factors that can make medical treatment a real challenge.

The breadth of symptoms and complaints that musicians present to specialists is wide indeed. There's a range of psychological and emotional disorders such as performance anxiety and depression. "We often deal with illnesses that affect playing but that can't be easily corrected," says Ostwald. "They may involve depression, or be related to competition, despair about careers, or marital problems." Performance anxiety, with its shakes and weak spells and nausea, is common to many kinds of performers. Some physicians report success with beta blockers to curb performance anxiety, although they worry that too many players come to use the drug by obtaining pills from other players. They also caution that when stage fright becomes so pervasive that it crops up during rehearsal and every time the player begins to play, other factors are at work that should be treated with counseling.

Today the most pressing need for enlightened care, and for future research, involves those unique and unusual elements of playing that take a specific toll on the body. Many pains and injuries are part of a given instrument's unique signature, like neck calluses and damage to the left arm and hand that violin players often develop. Bass players and cellists have more than their fair share of back problems from bending. And fingering and bow work common to nearly all string players makes them susceptible to two conditions prompted by so-called "overuse": carpal and cubital tunnel syndromes—inflammation of the wrist or elbow joint to a point where the swelling interferes with the ligaments, nerves, and muscles that pass through the tiny tunnels. The problem leads to pain, tingling, and even paralysis. Uncorrected, it can result in permanent nerve damage.

Then there are the more unusual problems. Skin irritations, including cysts and rashes, can evolve from either the pressure of the instrument against the skin, or substances such as varnishes on the instrument's surface. Also, many players develop hearing problems, both from sitting in a high-volume orchestra and from the volume of music they themselves are making.

Despite the common threads, physicians are loath to offer general advice to help avoid performance injuries, with the exception of urging players to maintain good overall health through proper diet, rest, and exercise, and always to warm up properly before playing. Beyond that, each case calls for its own prescription. And most insist that both musician and instrument pay a visit to the doctor's office for a precise investigation of what is going on.

If the problem is something like tendinitis or carpal tunnel syndrome, "Invariably, you have to stop playing for a short time," says Dr. David Rosenthal, who is both a violist and a physical medicine specialist from Morristown, Pennsylvania. "When you've got a highly inflamed area, you've got to put it to rest."

But as acute symptoms diminish, specialists design more specific treatments and suggestions for returning their patients back to playing. Sometimes it means prescribing a splint for the wrist, or a slow, gradual return to playing after a hiatus. There may be need of elaborate exercises designed to warm up and stretch specific joints and muscles before attempting to play. Brandfonbrener's research has convinced her that some finger injuries are caused by unusually lax joints; exercises to strengthen tiny muscles seem to help some players. Sometimes the physicians work with the player and even a player's teacher to try to adapt the player's posture or form to reduce stress. Occasionally they build special attachments that brace the instrument or relieve a player's sore neck or shoulder from strain, at least during practice. Others advocate techniques like yoga, the Feldenkrais method of movement, or the Alexander Technique. Says Westminster Choir College instructor Phyllis Lehrer, "Players must become more aware of their bodies and hidden pockets of tension."

Some players swear by chiropractors. Among performing arts medicine specialists, that invites an age-old debate between MDs and practitioners of joint and spinal manipulation. However, even Brandfonbrener acknowledges, "I do think we can all learn from chiropractors that there seems to be a big benefit to patients when we physically lay our hands on them."

As in many other aspects of medicine, the question of surgery is often intensely debated. Sometimes a surgery that repairs the average individual's functioning is insufficient to make a musician whole again. Denver cellist Melanie Burrell recalls the two years it took her to recover from hand surgery that was considered "simple." "I went to a top specialist and it was simple surgery, but it was designed for people with pounding injuries—jackhammer operators and butchers. If I were one of those people, I would have recovered immediately. But the minute and fast motions we develop can be disrupted very easily." Music medicine specialists typically say they first try rest and other remedies before resorting to surgery.

Rosenthal's rule of thumb for figuring out whether it's time for a musician to seek help is when the pain or ache persists for more than an hour after play. "It is not normal to have pain all night."

But even though musicians are emerging from the pain and anxiety closet, seeking medical help is still not a decision most make easily. Putting yourself out of action, even for a short while, affects more than just your career, notes San Antonio Symphony violinist Deborah Torch. "It puts pressure on your colleagues, too. They have to cover for you or put up with someone who's not a regular member of the orchestra." But as research begins to isolate better the causes and preferred treatments for musicians' maladies, players will likely be back in action faster, and may even be better players in the long run.

Nurturing wellness among young string players isn't such a stretch.

-James Reel

Staying Healthy

2

By James Reel

YOU'RE YOUNG; you're indestructible, right? You're a musician. You're not going to get hurt practicing, right? It's not as if you were playing football. Oh sure, maybe you've heard older professional musicians complaining about pain, numbness, inflammation, and muscle spasms. Last spring, for example, members of the Boston Symphony Orchestra were hurting so much that they asked their music director, James Levine, to ease up on the rehearsal schedule and to program shorter concerts.

But those are people who've been playing for decades. You're basically just getting started. You're invincible, right?

Wrong. You're never too young to get hurt. Forty to sixty percent of music students report suffering some sort of pain or injury. One study found that the chief physical complaints of music students arose from overuse (as you become more fatigued, you lose some of your sense of pain, which is not good) and tension. Behind these was a general lack of physical conditioning.

Lisa Britsch has seen it happen for years. Back when she was teaching high school orchestra, she had one student who would come in every Tuesday and say, "I can't play. It hurts ever since I played in youth symphony last night."

Britsch was puzzled. "I knew the youth symphony director, and he didn't let kids play in pain," she says. "There had to be something else going on."

That student inspired Britsch to look into ways to help teen musicians avoid chronic pain, or at least get help for it. Today she's a graduate student in the music education program at Michigan State University.

"Playing in pain is not OK," she warns. "If something hurts, something's wrong."

Have Healthy Habits

Britsch says that one big cause of trouble is failing to warm up properly before practice or performance. Another, especially among college students, is practicing too much. "Injuries happen when there's a sudden increase of practice, students don't work their way into it, and just plunge into practice before a recital," she says.

Many music teachers who've never dealt with pain themselves aren't sure how to spot problems in their students and offer help, Britsch says. One teacher who definitely is up on the subject is Judith Palac, one of Britsch's professors at Michigan State University. Healthy music habits have become one of her specialties.

"The first thing you have to do to avoid injury," Palac says, "is develop healthy habits overall. Some musical kids tend to be bookish and don't do sports, but sports can be great for musicians. Swimming is best, because it's not only a cardiovascular exercise; it also increases strength and flexibility by stretching. It's also a tension reducer, and it's about the least dangerous sport. You can't really hurt yourself swimming."

Palac says you don't have to get involved in the usual jock

activities if you don't want to. "Fencing, ballroom dancing, anything that gets the heart rate up and gets you toned up is helpful," she says. Avoid volleyball, though; that's dangerous to the fingers. Weight lifting isn't the best idea, either, she says, especially if it's done for body building rather than general toning. "Weight lifting for body building shortens and thickens the muscle fiber," she points out. "For music-making, you want muscle fibers to lengthen, to support better movement and increase flexibility."

Watch Your Posture

When it's time to practice or perform, one of the most important things to think about is posture. "Posture isn't just standing up straight," Palac says. "It's more like dynamic balance, and teens don't have it. Their legs grow faster than their arms, and their trunk muscles are the last to develop, so they have less trunk strength. Very often they're hunched over for good reasons, and at that age the body changes all the time, so it's like they're working with a new body every day."

All you can do to contend with this is to be very conscious of your posture every time you work with your instrument. But before you pick up that violin or cello, you need to warm up and stretch—which are two different things.

"With my students," says Palac, "we warm up every day by doing the hokey-pokey or walking in a circle or something that will get the blood flowing and warm up the muscles away from the instrument. If you're starting cold, you need to warm up before you stretch the muscles. Then stretch for a few minutes before rehearsal, and you should also stretch a little in the middle or at the end of rehearsal, because muscle fibers shorten up and get thicker when they're fatigued; if we stretch them out at the end of rehearsal, they'll be less likely to cramp the next day."

Palac and Britsch know perfectly well that you might think this is burdensome, tedious, or terminally uncool. But paying attention to techniques that will keep you from getting injured will pay off, and not just in music. "The number one cause of death for adolescents is failure to use safety devices like seatbelts and helmets," says Britsch. "They're not into preventative safety, so maybe it's asking a lot to get them to warm up before practice. But let me tell you, my fourteen-year-old is the only kid in the neighborhood who wears a bicycle helmet. I'm not taking any chances."

Smooth and Easy

OK, so you're ready to sit down and play. You've warmed up and you're thinking about your posture. You have your instrument and bow in hand. Now what?

"First, move smoothly," Palac advises. "When you throw a baseball, you wind up, then throw, and then follow through. When you play an instrument you have to maintain good movement patterns and think about preparation; if you don't, you can injure your muscles and soft tissues and joints.

"Then there's leverage. Use as much muscular force as necessary, but as little as possible. Some kids push down on the string and push down on the bow rather than using muscles to produce weight, not force. And never pound your fingers on the fingerboard."

"Stay in the middle range of motion, which is the healthiest place for every joint," Palac continues. "With wrists that means the wrist is practically straight out from the arm, not bent too much. You should play so your body looks like arcs and spirals, not squares and trapezoids."

"Balance: spread your weight evenly across the base of your body, whether you're sitting or standing. And don't hike one shoulder higher than the other. Since we all go forward all the time in string playing, because we're reaching around something, it's good to stretch your arms and back backward when you're finished playing, to counteract that forward motion."

During practice, manage your workload by taking breaks. Palac recommends at least standing and bending back for twenty seconds every half hour. If your practice lasts longer than an hour, it's good to take a ten-minute break for every hour of work. "This seems like a lot to think about," Palac admits, "but if we start out this way, pretty soon it becomes part of our natural routine."

Then there's the question of having the right stuff. Not talent or dedication, but stuff around you to help you avoid hurting yourself. Like the right kind of chair. It should be tall enough that your upper legs are parallel to the ground, with your lower legs aiming for the floor at a ninety-degree angle. You most certainly shouldn't sit with your knees above your hip joints.

And don't forget the stuff that attaches to your instrument. "A lot of students get tired of looking for the right fit and just try to conform their bodies to their instrument rather than the other way around," says Palac.

Cellists, for example, may need shorter or longer or even curved endpins for better balance. Violinists and violists need well-fitted chin rests and shoulder rests.

Young students should move on to bigger instruments with caution. "In terms of muscle strain, it's better for the instrument to be a little small than too large," says Palac.

Take Your Medicine

If you do develop pain, don't panic. Sometimes starting a new technique will cause temporary aches. But if the pain persists, talk to your teacher. Rest more, which at first means do only what you can do and stop when it hurts. There's some disagreement over whether to apply ice or heat to the problem area, but Palac says, "Ice for ten minutes an hour can't hurt you."

Go to your doctor, and tell the doc exactly where it hurts and what you're doing when the pain starts. Even music teachers and doctors may not be completely familiar with the injuries that arise from playing, so you may need to visit a specialist in performing arts medicine—or, if that's too far away, a good sports medicine doctor. (This may cost more time and money than seeing a general physician, but your problem will likely be solved in only one or two visits.)

Then follow through on whatever the doctor tells you to do. If you're supposed to take an anti-inflammatory like ibuprofen for two weeks, do it for the entire two weeks. Don't stop early when you start feeling better; even if the pain is gone the underlying inflammation may not be completely eliminated.

To avoid trouble in the future, Palac suggests working with good body-use practitioners. "Alexander Technique and Pilates teachers are good with the mechanics of the human body," she says. "They can help you use your body better so you don't get injured again."

Muscles that are tight, weak, and untoned are more injury-prone than strong, flexible, and resilient muscles.

-Janet Horvath

The Ten *Dos* and *Don'ts* 3

By Janet Horvath

Ten *Dos*

1. **Do warm up.** Warm muscles are more efficient, strong, and resilient. Muscles that are overused, fatigued, and under-conditioned are more tense and require more work for a demanding task. Start with several slow and smooth stretches away from the instrument. Start slowly and easily at the instrument. Long, slow shifts are good, and then slow scales. If it is cold outside, warm yourself before playing.

2. **Do take breaks.** Ten minutes per hour minimum is a good guide. Let your arms hang down for a few seconds after a difficult passage. After tremolo or *fortissimo* passages, move your right thumb in circles or stretch it out gently to release any tension.

3. **Do keep your shoulders down and your back straight.** Lifting shoulders, turning or twisting your torso, or leaning to the left or right contributes to muscle strain and may lead to injury.

4. **Do sit with good posture.** Keep your weight forward and on your feet, and your feet on the floor. Keep your head upright and in a neutral position. Dropping your head forward or turning to either side tightens neck and shoulder muscles and could also compress surrounding nerve ends, causing headaches, disc problems, and eye strain.

5. **Do some stress-reducing relaxation activity and get regular exercise.** Yoga, stretching, swimming, Alexander Technique, and massage are all good preventative activities. These can help to keep tension from building up. Muscles that are tight, weak, and untoned are more injury-prone than strong, flexible, and resilient muscles.

6. **Do take one day off per week.** You'll benefit from a day spent simply relaxing, thinking about the music, and getting refreshed for tomorrow's playing.

7. **Do be easier on yourself when you are under stress or when you are overtired.** Your body will be more tense and at risk for injury when you are preparing for a big recital or audition, starting a new job, moving to a new city, or when you're trying a new instrument or switching teachers. These are times to be careful about long hours of intense playing. Stress can manifest itself as muscle tension, often localized in the trapezius muscles in the back. Many players raise their shoulders and tense neck and shoulder muscles when under duress. When you're stressed or overtired, take more breaks, take more time to warm up, do neck stretches and shoulder rolls more often, and practice more mindfully.

8. **Do move.** Sitting very still builds up tension. During long hours of playing, take time to wiggle, roll your thumbs, get up, roll your shoulders, stretch your neck from side to side, pull your shoulders back, and reach up to the ceiling. For violinists and violists, untwist your left arm. Some of these movements can even be done onstage during concerts.

9. **Do breathe deeply.** When we're nervous, we tend to breathe very shallowly, or even hold our breath. Our muscles then may not get the oxygen that they need. In fact, they may begin to shake. During rests in the music, concentrate on taking several deep breaths. If you shake, you may be tense somewhere. Hold your breath, tense everything, and then release.

10. **Do practice away from the instrument.** Mental preparation is very important, and it's especially helpful for memorization. Listen to a recording and study the scores or piano parts of your repertoire. Visualize performing well. Silence that doubting voice inside of you by giving yourself positive suggestions, such as "I am calm," or "I sound wonderful," rather than "What if I mess up this shift?" or "I'm sure to have a memory slip."

Ten *Don'ts*

1. **Don't ignore pain.** Pain is an indicator. Your body is trying to tell you something. Stop playing, ice the area, take some time off, and try to analyze what may have caused the problem. Don't forget to consider nonmusical activities as well as technique at the instrument.

2. **Don't be macho.** Don't try to practice for hours and hours. Consistency is more important than marathons. Don't practice everything *fortissimo* and up to tempo. Pace yourself by practicing at slower tempos and softer dynamics.

3. **Don't practice mindlessly.** Use a tape recorder to practice with critical ears. Analyze and isolate problems in your repertoire rather than going over and over a passage. Have a realistic plan that you'd like to accomplish before you start practicing. Don't play through pieces all the time. Vary the types of music you practice. Physically, you use different muscles for different kinds of passages or repertoire, so you actually give yourself a break when you switch to another type of piece. It is more effective to limit time on a difficult passage and to return to it later in the day than to keep playing it over and over.

4. **Don't ignore chewed up fingers.** Either your bridge is too high or you're pressing your fingers too hard or both. It doesn't take hammering to press strings down. Only the playing finger should be in playing tension; in other words, don't hold your fingers down. Release all nonplaying fingers.

5. **Don't jump into playing a full schedule after a vacation, after being sick, or especially after an injury.** Take time to get back into shape gradually. It's better to play for short periods more often throughout the day than to practice in long chunks. Start with ten to fifteen minutes. Increase the number of ten-minute practice periods per day before increasing the length of time.

6. **Don't say "yes" to everything.** Especially at summer music festivals or in a particularly stimulating environment, it's easy to get in over your head. Be realistic about how many chamber groups you can be in or how many performances you can do. Don't schedule so tightly that you arrive breathless for a rehearsal with no time to warm up.

7. **Don't cram or show up unprepared for a rehearsal.** Try to allow yourself enough time to prepare your auditions or recitals. When this is impossible, try to program wisely. Don't program several works that are new to you. Sight-reading does not allow you to anticipate motions. Your body motions are jerky and sudden rather than smooth and prepared as they are when you know what's coming. Sudden quick motions can lead to injury. Try to look ahead in the music and focus on relaxed, flowing motions.

8. **Don't play on an instrument that is out of adjustment.** Make sure your instrument is properly repaired so it responds easily. Cellists: lower your bridges. Make sure neck thickness and angle are to proper specifications. Violinists: adjust your chin rests and shoulder pads to suit you. They can even be custom made. Bass players: adjust stools and endpin heights. Violists: look for a smaller, lighter instrument, if possible. Avoid very heavy, clumsy, or inflexible bows.

9. **Don't ignore conditions around you.** Don't play if you have no room and you are cramped. Don't position your stand so you have to crane your neck to see it; don't sit so you have to struggle to see the conductor. Avoid playing in cold places or where there is a draft. Try to adjust the conditions around you so that you can be as comfortable as possible. Don't wear tight clothing; this will also tend to cramp you physically.

10. **Don't panic if something hurts.** Some aches and pains are inevitable. Take a day off and don't worry about it. A short rest usually takes care of most minor aches. Learn your limitations and the danger signals. If you are worried, ask someone who knows.

Upon returning to playing after stretching, the musician is more comfortable and therefore more productive.
-Carrie Booher, Joanne Horner, and Derek Noll

It's a Stretch! 4

AN OCCUPATIONAL-THERAPY PERSPECTIVE ON PLAYER HEALTH AND WELLNESS

By Carrie Booher, Joanne Horner, and Derek Noll

FREQUENTLY THE EVENING NEWS warns of repetitive-strain injuries (RSI) and the plight of the office worker. Sitting at a computer for long periods of time, day in and day out, gradually increases the risk of carpal tunnel syndrome. Yet injuries related to careers in the performing arts are rarely discussed. According to the 1993 edition of *Vital Statistics*, "Seventy-five percent of professional musicians suffered serious injuries as a result of their career." While recent injury data for performing artists is scarce and is not listed by specific instrument, acknowledgment can be found in such publications as *Medical Problems of Performing Artists*, printed quarterly by the Performing Arts Medicine Association.

Musicians have a wealth of healthcare options within traditional medicine disciplines, including nursing, dentistry, occupational and physical therapies, as well as such nontraditional medicine specialties as Alexander Technique, trigger point therapy, chiropractic, acupuncture, Feldenkrais, yoga, rolfing, and Pilates. Performing artists face so many choices for health care and prevention that it is important for each individual to recognize the viability of every option. Occupational therapy efficacy studies have been conducted with other work-related injury populations, and the results of these studies may be applied to the performing arts as well.

Lifestyle Redesign

During a recent presentation about the benefits of occupational therapy for the performing musician held at Chatham College in Pittsburgh, students were polled regarding their experiences with pain during performance. All twenty-five students reported experiencing pain during practice or performance at some time. The class and presenters discussed how pain is often ignored in everyday life, since people in today's high-pressure world simply do not have time to acknowledge pain. After reviewing sobering statistics regarding musician injury, the presenters, a group of occupational therapy graduate students, offered creative solutions for the prevention of pain and repetitive-strain injuries.

An occupational therapist (OT) can evaluate a client's habits and routines to identify those that are health promoting and those that are health compromising, and then make recommendations for a lifestyle redesign. For a musician, a therapist may suggest building in frequent breaks (such as a ten minute rest for every fifty minutes spent practicing) to make time for stretching, reducing the stress of long hours of sustained posture. Also, splints can serve as both a preventative and recovery measure in the treament of pain and injury; an OT can explain the freedom of movement that is available while wearing specific splints.

Once an injury has occurred, the emphasis shifts to rehabilitation of the injury through strength-building exercises and engaging in daily occupational therapy. For example, a musician's performance can be made therapeutic by using a weighted instrument to increase endurance in anticipation of a particularly long concert. For a client whose injury has resulted in permanently diminished function, an OT can adapt the environment, equipment, or technique to meet a particular challenge.

During the Chatham College presentation, presenters used a built-up bow handle with a padded grip as an example of an adaptation. Made of soft foam, this bow allows a violinist with arthritis to play with less pain and reduced grip strength.

Try This at Home

What can a musician do in terms of physical exercise to avoid jeopardizing his or her future? Start by taking a proactive approach to managing and reducing existing pain and preventing further injury. There are many different ways a musician can achieve and maintain good health.

One of the most effective is through stretching and hand massage exercises coupled with frequent rest breaks. Stretching exercises can enhance flexibility and circulation, reduce fatigue, and increase endurance, thereby minimizing the risk of injury. The exercises take just five minutes to perform and can be integrated into a musician's practice session. Upon returning to playing after stretching, the musician is more comfortable, and therefore more productive. Stretching can also reduce the risk of carpal tunnel syndrome, a repetitive-strain injury caused by sustaining poor wrist posture over time. Many musicians are susceptible to this

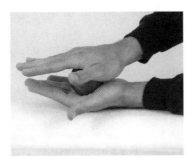

ON A ROLL: A soft rubber ball can help with simple stretching exercises.

injury due to the awkward hand positions required to hold an instrument while playing. Stretching is also beneficial for those players who are not yet experiencing pain, as it may prevent injury.

Be proactive about prevention. Seek out a health care provider who can provide the latest information about traditional and alternative treatments, recommend dietary guidelines, and describe appropriate procedures for music-related injuries. And it is important to ask the health care provider if there is research to validate the efficacy of the proposed treatment. Ask questions and stay current with new research regarding your specific needs to protect your career as a performing artist.

The available evidence suggests that regular stretching enhances performance and reduces injuries.

-John Jerome

The Pleasures of Stretching

5

EXCERPTED FROM
STAYING SUPPLE: THE BOUNTIFUL PLEASURES OF STRETCHING

By John Jerome

TO STAY SUPPLE you must maintain the health and resilience of your connective tissue and the muscle it contains. Regular stretching helps maintain that health and resilience. If you are an athlete or a regular exerciser, this advice probably isn't new to you, although you may have been asked to take it on faith. Nobody ever quite says what stretching is or what it does. I'd like to rectify that.

Stretching instructions used to speak only of muscle, but a wave of recent stretching information has changed the emphasis to the connective tissue. Both are correct, but it helps to keep in mind the connective tissue, more than the muscle, when you stretch. If you think only of stretching muscle, you're not as likely to find stretching a satisfying and fruitful activity.

When you stretch, you place muscle and connective tissue under a lengthening tension. To stretch effectively you must relax the muscles while you're stretching them. The resistance to the stretch should come from the elasticity of the tissues, not from the contraction of the muscle. An ideal stretching program would regularly take all of the articulated segments of the body through their full range of motion, but that's asking a little much even from full-time athletes; most people settle for consistent, regular stretching of the muscles and tendons that work the major joints, or those that are hardest used.

The available evidence suggests that regular stretching enhances performance and reduces injuries. Stretching also reduces the soreness that results from the work, and speeds recovery. It helps resist the gradual shortening and tightening of tissue that otherwise sets in from both over- and underuse, reducing the discomfort and slowing the progressive loss of capacity that accompanies this tightening. And stretching helps neurologically, keeping the proprioceptive system tuned, the muscles' tone and reactivity balanced, one's sense of personal dimension sharp and accurate.

Stretching accomplishes all these things mostly by restoring freshness. It is assumed to help straighten out the mechanical results of fatigue, physically reorganizing muscle and connective tissue fibers into their proper order—training them, in effect, to seek and maintain their optimum length. It also helps wash out the chemical residues of fatigue—the acids and other metabolic wastes that impair healing, slow the restoration of energy supplies, and hasten the mechanical shortening of tissue.

In addition, stretching seems to help quiet the neuromuscular "noise" that leaves muscles with those knots, spasms, and kernels of pain that you can't quite relax, that your best intentions can't reach. Physiology is strikingly vague about what these knots are and what causes them, but as surely as muscles contract in response to neural signals, they must fail to decontract because they're still getting some kind of residual signaling: noise. (This signaling is produced in part by the irritation caused by waste product. Pain is one kind of noise.) Stretching should interrupt those unresolved contractions mechanically, helping restore normal function. This has not been proved, only observed.

One explanation offered for the knots and spasms is fibrosis—abnormal formation of fibrous tissue, another poorly understood phenomenon. Injured muscle fibers have limited capacity to repair themselves; any large deficit is replaced by connective tissue. The smaller, microscopic tissue ruptures that are a natural product of hard use, called micro trauma, also must be healed. How much of that repair is laid down as muscle, and how much as scar tissue, also is not clear. Muscle tissue, connective tissue, and scar tissue are three distinct categories to physiologists, but are not necessarily so clearly distinguished in real life. Hands-on therapists tend to suspect some kind of fibrosis as the culprit in muscle shortening: a literal turning of muscle fiber into connective fiber. It seems to happen mostly near the muscle ends, where muscle tissue gradually turns into tendon. Hard use develops muscle tissue, but it may also slowly shift the area that divides muscle from tendon, not entirely distinct in any case, away from the joint and toward the muscle, reducing strength and increasing the risk of tendon injury. Athletes and trainers describe a muscle in that condition as "tight," a sign that it is overused. Stretching has the unusual capacity to help turn scar tissue into more functional connective tissue. It helps resist any such shift.

This function implies another, much larger, role of stretching in maintaining suppleness. If you've ever had a limb in a cast, you know how dramatically muscle tissue wastes away from lack of movement. Movement, or contraction, is what maintains muscle health. Tension-stretching seems similarly to help maintain connective tissue health. Without regular contraction, muscle tissue atrophies; without regular tension, connective tissue loses its suppleness.

Internal Stretching

There is one aspect of stretching about which all are in agreement: you want to relax as much as possible the muscle tissue you're stretching. Stretching should be an aid to relaxation in every way, a de-tensifier, a gentle wringing out of all strictures and contractions, muscular or otherwise.

A powerful tool for relaxation is the deep breath. Most presentations of stretching emphasize breathing as an adjunct to every stretch, often venturing into anatomical looniness to do so. ("Breathe into the stretch." "Direct your breathing into your calf muscle as you stretch it." "Breathe through the top of your head.") If the image works for you—if you can follow the advice without giggling— then it's probably a useful tool.

It's probably a good idea even if you do break into giggles. Norman Cousins points out that laughter is a way of taking your internal organs out for a jog. Laughing stretches the diaphragm, just as a good deep breath does. Smiling and laughing give the facial musculature a good stretch. (Yoga has you making horrific faces to accomplish the same thing.) There are plenty of other non-musculoskeletal aspects of our physiology for which a good stretch is an effective toner, if you can just figure a way of getting at them to stretch them out.

Deep breathing is one of the best. A good deep breath may be the most powerful natural tranquilizer available to us, the system's own miracle drug, the universal palliative. All creatures call upon its restorative powers. Horses and dogs definitely do; I think I've even heard a chicken sigh. In times of stress we air-breathers want at least one chest-expanding, inhale-plus-exhale before plunging into the action, whether the action is swinging at a fastball, skiing an icy mogul field, or playing the opening bars of a sonata. Experienced performers take such breaths consciously, deliberately calling on deep breathing's powers of relaxation. When the circumstances are severe enough, when we are sufficiently uncertain about impending events, the same settling controlled inhale/exhale will be wrenched from us, whatever our level of experience. The body, in its wisdom, demands it.

In yoga almost as much attention is devoted to breath as to stretching. Special ways of breathing are aimed at centering and calming the body, to free the mind for higher pursuits. Stress reduction clinics often start with breath control before they go on to all the Type A and Type B stuff. Counting to ten when you lose your temper, folk wisdom's sound advice, is in part a delay to give you a couple of breaths to get hold of yourself.

Stretching It Out

You already know how to stretch. You're an expert at it. Even if you live a completely sedentary life, you stretch every day, habitually and safely. You stretch whenever your body demands it, which is usually when you haven't been moving around enough for the body's tastes. You also stretch after you've been moving too much.

You stretch automatically, reflexively. When you get up from your stand, your theater seat, even from your comfortable bed, you stretch out exactly those parts that want stretching the most; they tell you to stretch them, and you comply. In order to ease your stiffness, you move things, slowly, more or less gently, pulling taut your lower back, trunk, shoulders, neck. Doing so usually makes you yawn, which stretches your jaw and face. It makes you groan with pleasure. You stretch what feels good, for as long as it feels good to do so. This rule was given to me by my son, and in fact is the only rigid rule you'll find me laying down. It bears repeating: Stretch only what feels good, for as long as it feels good to do so. Afterward, what you will feel is relief.

All the principles of a successful stretching program are contained above. To increase the pleasure, and the relief, you'll only be varying those principles, expanding their application. That takes a little experimentation, a little

little feeling around in the musculoskeletal system to find what works best for you. You may also have to learn to think a little differently about what you're doing. You have to learn to experience your body as a single piece. Try an experiment: Let your hand rest on some solid surface. Begin pushing down as if you're trying to push that surface through the floor. Slowly increase the pressure. Feel the muscular contraction work its way up, starting at your wrist, progressing up the forearm and the back of the upper arm. (Feel how slack the biceps muscle has gone, almost toneless, as you tighten the triceps: that's reciprocal inhibition, another reflex.)

You feel this progressive contraction first as a stiffening of the wrist joint and then the elbow, the smaller muscles locking the joint into immobility before the larger muscles are brought into play and real force is exerted. If you continue to bear down, you'll draw tight a complex arrangement of muscles and tendons around the shoulder joint, locking it tight as well. Continue, and as you run out of available increase from the obvious large muscles of arm and shoulder, you will engage musculature of the chest and back, searching for ways to apply your body weight to that downward-pressing palm.

This small experiment demonstrates several things about the stretching process. It illuminates, for example, the intricacy of the structures involved in generating real force. The large muscles—biceps, triceps, thighs, hamstrings, calves—dominate athletic thinking, but they can't be put to work until complex systems of smaller muscle-tendon units have braced and aligned the frame and properly set the joints. We often direct our training and our maintenance to the major muscles, assuming that the peripheral structures will take care of themselves. But soreness and injuries occur in muscles we don't perceive as major, and do so perhaps more frequently than they do in the larger, stronger structures. Those "minor" injuries, as many musicians can attest, put us out of action as effectively as do problems with the big stuff.

HEALTHY STRING PLAYING

It's also worth noting how that ripple of contraction spreads from your palm throughout your body. As you keep increasing the downward force, the sensation is as if you're drawing tight a net, one that extends from your palm right on throughout the rest of your body, head to toes. You won't feel it pull tight everywhere, even if you really get serious about increasing the force, but apply enough pressure and you will feel it pull in all directions. You can trace it around joints, across your back, even down the backs of your legs. This is the network that ties you into a single anatomical piece. This network of muscle and connective tissue is what you want to learn to stretch back out to length.

Also worth considering is how you search around in your anatomy for ways to increase the force. It's almost as if you are trying and discarding various elements—muscles, angles, ways of getting an anatomical purchase on the problem to find what works best. You'll find yourself using this same kind of conscious search through the anatomy as you invent new ways to stretch. With it you'll find no end of new places, new parts of yourself, that are accessible to stretching, that in fact cry out for it. If there is a single tool that makes for a successful stretching program, it is this level of attention. Zen Buddhists must be talking about something very like this when they speak of "one-pointedness." (When hauling water, the Zen master says, just haul water; when chopping wood, just chop wood. That is, don't haul around your problems with the IRS, don't chop up your boss along with the wood. When stretching, just stretch, but pay attention.)

The clearer your sense of your anatomy, the more pleasure and relaxation you will get out of stretching. If you only stretch reflexively, unconsciously, as when you rise from your desk, you're working with mere tissue. If you stretch consciously, reading the sensations and using them to guide your movements, you are held—for brief moments, anyway—in the present tense. Spending time in the present tense, instead of restlessly re-evaluating the past or worrying about the future, is the deepest rest there is. That, too, is a kind of one-pointedness, a way of capturing a bit of time for yourself and getting maximum use from it.

The Pleasure Part

You want to hold each stretch just as long as it holds your attention. When your mind begins to wander, stretch something else. You definitely don't want to rush. You want a relaxed and leisurely approach, a sense of taking the pressure off. Stretching should, in effect, unplug your phone. It should be a signal to your brain: "Let go, damn it!" Step out of your Type A life (or the Type A aspects of your life) for a little while. Drop your tensed shoulders, ease off that cramp at the back of your neck. Kick off your metaphorical shoes, even if you're already barefoot.

Relaxation is what you're after; you pursue it by applying, then letting go of, tension. You are as interested in relaxing the contractibility of the muscle as you are in pulling taut the elasticity of its tendons. Focusing your mind on what's happening, making sure you've let everything go in the muscle does take a little while, in every stretch. This is time you fill with gradually increasing tension. (How do you relax and apply tension at the same time? You relax the area you're stretching, and stretch it by pulling on it with other muscles. When you stretch your arms wide upon arising, for example, you contract the muscles across your back and shoulders in order to stretch your chest and the front of your shoulders.) It's not a bad idea to hold a given tension, then take up the slack. Your guide shouldn't be a fixed number of seconds, however, but the sensation you're getting from the elements you're stretching. If you're stretching your hamstring, you should feel the fibers pull tight behind the knee at first, then, as you increase pressure, from heel to butt along the back of your leg. Pay attention to that progression. I find that if I really con-centrate, I can almost always find a little something else in there to relax, another fraction of an inch of movement to pick up, another notch forward. That conscious relaxation, that focus on the area you're stretching, seems to do as much good as the actual lengthening of the tissue.

Reverse the experiment described earlier. Relax the downward force on your palm, and push your shoulder and elbow forward so you bend your wrist back, until you feel the connective tissue in the palm and the underside of your wrist begin to pull tight. Push your elbow farther forward and the tension works its way from wrist to palm to fingers to fingertips. This is an area of tissue that usually does not get stretched, which makes it easier to pay fresh attention to it. You want to figure out how to make stretching it pleasurable.

You do that by experimenting with the level of tension. At the first level of tightness it has a familiar muscular feel to it; as you increase the tension it begins to feel as if nerves are involved: more tingly, electrical. There is a continuum of sensation from the initial tightness, relief of which is purely pleasurable, right on into pain. It is a continuum with which you want to become intimately familiar. In the earliest stages, you are taking out the slack, pulling things back out to their normal resting length. As you increase the tension, you begin to work the tissue, to pull fibers into alignment. That's when you begin to stimulate the biochemical processes that lead to actual growth, strengthening, improvement. Think of it that way: you're not yanking on the tissue or even trying literally to lengthen it, you're organizing it.

Apply too much tension and you begin to disrupt the tissue's own micro trauma of hard use. Your guide to proper tension is pleasure: you want to learn to take the tension up the scale of intensity, without tipping over into the pain that signals that healing will have to take place. You never want to stretch anything harder than you stretch your arms and back when you climb out of bed in the morning. (If you feel you have to stretch it hard, you haven't got the correct angle of pull. Feel around, try some other angles, find a way to put gentle tension on it in a controlled manner.)

Stretching your hand and forearm is a useful test for familiarizing yourself with these sensations. If you are a pianist or violinist, or otherwise use those parts of your anatomy long and hard, you may already be inclined to stretch them out. (If not, you may find you can do so more effectively by pressing your hands palm to palm, or locking your fingers, palm outward, and straightening your elbows, in the time-honored pianist's limbering up routine.) But leaning on one hand on a table and pressing the elbow forward to stretch fingers, palm, wrist, and forearm is a nicely controllable way to experiment with stretching tensions and their sensations.

Once you have a sense of the level of tension that begins to work the tissue, try twisting from side to side at the wrist, or rolling your elbow from one side to the other. Rotate the bones gently against each other. This stretch extends the wrist; try flexing it, stretching it in the opposite direction, reaching back toward the elbow with the fingertips. You're working an extremely complex structure: nineteen major bones in the fingers and hand alone, eight more in the wrist, two in the forearm, all tied together with distinctive ligaments, worked by separate sets of muscles for flexing and for extending, each muscle attached to the bone by tendons on each end.

All of these structures need movement to maintain their health. Work them too little and the connective tissue begins to deteriorate, the joints to lose their mobility (the onset of degenerative joint disease); work them too much and they accumulate the biochemical and structural results of fatigue. They need the healthy tension of stretching to set things right again. Musicians, artists, even assembly-line workers who use their hands very hard, suffer crippling overuse injuries when they lose the suppleness of their hands. Careful warm up by flexing, mostly in the form of gentle stretching, is how suppleness is maintained. A little exploration will quickly turn up half a dozen other ways to flex these intricate structures. One of the best is simply to spread your fingers wide, stiffening and extending hands and fingers. Hold the extension stiff for a few seconds, and you'll begin to feel muscular fatigue too, and you can begin to compare that sensation with the sensation of a good stretch. You'll want to be able to distinguish between the two. People who don't stretch seem to have trouble doing so.

In fact, if we were trained to use our minds and bodies
properly, pain and injury could be almost completely erased
from the process of creating music.

-Julie Lyonn Lieberman

You Are Your Instrument 6

MUSCULAR CHALLENGES IN PRACTICE AND PERFORMANCE

By Julie Lyonn Lieberman

ACCORDING TO *The New England Journal of Medicine*
(January 26, 1989), almost half of all musicians experience
playing-related medical problems, and string players are the
most commonly affected. Tension, misuse, and awkward body
positions combined with long hours of repetitive movement
account for most tension-related problems and injuries.

The economic pressures that come with being a musician
contribute to an overall level of tension; these pressures are
exacerbated by juries, auditions, and the demands of a note-
perfect performance for classical musicians, and the challenges
of attracting a new audience for improvising musicians. String
players have additional pressures: we must use each hand for
totally different activities with micro-perfect coordination
while creating each pitch from "out of nowhere."

After thirteen years of experimentation on myself and my
students, studying the body and mind in relationship to music-
making, and completing my newest book, *You Are Your
Instrument*, I am convinced that the incredibly high
percentage of muscle-related problems in musicians reflects an
imbalance in our music education system. In fact, if we were

trained to use our minds and bodies properly, pain and injury could be almost completely erased from the process of creating music.

A balanced education, or re-education for those of us who have already trained for many years, must include techniques for healthy practice and performance. Whether practicing, rehearsing, playing at a lesson, or performing, there are specific mental and physical actions that we can take to maintain a relaxed, fluidly alive technique without damaging our bodies.

During this process of learning how to use our bodies differently while playing, it is essential to resist other people's imagined or real agendas. You must be willing to speak up and change conditions that tend to lead to injury. By paying attention to your body's signals, you can make constant adjustments in your posture, instrument hold, use of your hands and arms, and mindset. Simple adjustments, such as slowing down or decreasing volume during practice sessions or rehearsals, or taking the steps needed to warm up at a lesson, can facilitate the sensitivity, objectivity, and mental focus required to make a shift to muscular fluidity. The motto "no pain, no gain" must change to "if it hurts, then I'm doing something wrong."

Since one of the largest causes of injury is repetitive activity that overuses the muscles, practicing for many hours a day can be detrimental to the body. The cumulative effect on the tissues can eventually exceed the body's physiological limits and can result in injury.

I have found that fifty percent of the time that musicians spend practicing is unnecessary, injurious, and wasted. Most practice can be accomplished mentally in far less time and with better results through the use of imaging. In fact, a lot of repetition is often done mindlessly, a crack through which injury can move in. Muscle memory is important but dangerous without concurrent mental awareness, and is often the first thing to go under performance pressure.

I use the terms *visualization* and *imaging* to differentiate between two specific right-brain functions. To experience the difference, sit comfortably, close your eyes, choose a piece of music, take a deep breath and relax. Imagine that you're in a movie theater watching a movie of yourself playing the piece. You are just a spectator. I call this process visualization. It's a valuable tool for performance preparation because you can create a picture of yourself playing beautifully, with self-confidence and muscular fluidity.

Imaging, on the other hand, involves your kinesthetic senses. Using that same piece of music, imagine playing each note as if you were moving your body the way you do when you play, but don't actually move. Stay relaxed, breathe deeply, and hear the music in your inner ear. This is the same mental process as in sexual fantasies (unless we play the role of the voyeur) or in deep relaxation techniques like, "imagine you're lying on a warm beach; hear the sound of the waves..."

To image, you employ your proprioceptive, aural, and analytic memory of the music. Imaging immediately highlights which parts of the piece present problems. While imaging, note that you tend to hold your breath or tighten up on the passages that you also struggle with when you're actually playing. Imaging gives you the chance to train yourself to play those passages with precision as well as with muscular fluidity and proper breathing.

Each time you image the piece of music before you play it again, you will increase your mastery. Eventually you can even image and play simultaneously so that all body movement originates from focused proprioceptive/aural imaging.

Julie Lyonn Lieberman

Muscle Balance

Through repetition, the body learns patterns of movement in whole phrases, e.g., if every time you play the second measure you hold your breath and stand on the sides of your feet, your nervous system links those sounds and movements into one phrase. Training yourself to use your body consciously as you play takes time and consistent awareness. But no matter how conscious you are, when certain movements and postures are repeated again and again, you gradually create an imbalance in your musculature. Unless you do other kinds of exercise before or after playing, your body is bound to protest from the stress.

You can provide muscle balance through a simple system of movements or exercises designed to compensate for repetitive movements and postures. For instance, if you play an instrument that requires a constant forward motion of the arms and body, any kind of exercise that opens the chest or presses the arms back will help balance the muscle groups involved. For instance, try lying on your stomach and stretching your arms over your head. Lift your arms straight back on an exhale. Repeat this five to ten times, slowly, inhaling each time you return your arms to the floor. Just about any form of exercise can be helpful as long as you don't strain, hold your breath, or do too much at once. Listen to your body. Use simple movement exercises to tone your muscles and get your blood flowing. Remember to take deep breaths while you move.

Rejuvenation and Healing

Rest is probably one of the best healers available. In addition to taking the time to participate in other activities, you can also structure constructive rest time into your practice. I use constructive rest to align my spine. I lie on the floor, with bent knees. As I lie there, I relax my muscles so that my breath moves deeply and naturally. Meanwhile, I image playing the music I was just practicing, adding any aspects that I left out during my "active" practice sessions. I also come up with images that will help specific passages or release tense patterns when I return to my instrument. On a particular string crossing, for instance, I turn my arm and hand into rubber. One passage I play like flowing water, another like a three-hundred-pound truck driver.

Bodywork can aid the healing process immeasurably. Bodywork sessions can enhance relaxation, reduce chronic muscular contraction, and increase circulation. Use them to nurture yourself and to learn new approaches you can apply to music making. In summary, remember to:

1. Monitor your body as you play.
2. Breathe deeply and consistently.
3. Exercise to stretch, strengthen, and balance muscles.
4. Be willing to stop and make the changes you need to support your health.
5. Use imaging to enhance muscle and auditory memory.

Music-making involves aural, tactile, and kinesthetic awareness. Conscious mental direction through conceptualizing and imaging can have an enormous impact on the way our bodies perform, as well as the degree of mental and physical effort we expend. The more we tune out, the greater the damage we incur. Our body-mind has an internal intelligence that we must learn to trust. Pain is a valuable signal. If we listen to it carefully with our finely trained musician's ears, it tells us how and where we are abusing ourselves. With commitment to the body's full participation, music-making can become pain-free, graceful, and fluidly alive.

Remember, you want to avoid a crack, not treat one.

-Yvonne Caruthers

Keeping Fingertip Cracks at Bay

7

By Yvonne Caruthers

LAST WINTER I was plagued by cracks on my fingertips to such an extent that I submitted a plea to *Strings* magazine (Q & A, April 1998), hoping that other readers would have more successful ideas than mine for combating the problem. Literally dozens responded to that question, and a number of those responses appeared in the July issue.

Many suggestions dealt with healing the cracks once they appear, but I'm trying to prevent them from occurring in the first place. I decided to talk to some medical professionals about the problem, and I hope the answers will help many of you avoid the pain associated with those nasty cracks.

I started with dermatologist Dr. John Reeves, of the University of Vermont in Burlington. "How can I prevent this skin problem?" I asked.

"First you need the correct parents," he said. "The dead-skin layer on top of the layer of live skin is different in genetically different people. Some people's dead-skin layer is supple and well lubricated. For others, it's brittle and less lubricated. Those people frequently have dry shins, chapped lips, and dry faces."

We string players are familiar with the layers of dead skin that build up on our fingers where we push down on our strings—they're calluses. According to Dr. Reeves, on some people the dead-skin layer is made of long chains of dead cells, and those long chains are fairly supple. People prone to dry skin have shorter chains of these cells; their chains are more likely to break apart. The live-skin layer underneath has no toughness; once exposed, it cracks and bleeds.

A type of oil contained in the cells themselves lubricates the dead skin layer. Said Dr. Reeves, "Imagine a new pair of leather shoes that are soft and supple. Then wash them about 25 times without oiling them between washes. They will dry out and crack. The same is true for your skin. If you wash away the oil faster than it can be replaced, then you have dry, cracking skin.

"For string players the problem is made worse because of friction caused by the fingers rubbing on the strings. Friction creates calluses, but it also fragments the top skin layer, so in effect you are sandpapering your already brittle skin. Exposure to rosin can make the problem worse too, since rosin is a very drying material. People with the same type of skin might not experience the same severity of problem if they only handle papers all day, but this condition is catastrophic for hairdressers, whose hands are always wet or in chemicals."

By this point in the conversation I felt doomed. Obviously I must not have chosen the right parents, and I rub my fingers on metal strings for hours at a time. One plus for me: I'm careful to hold my rosin by the cloth around it, so at least I'm not coating my calluses with rosin before I sandpaper them. Even so, my short-chain dead-skin layer is constantly being fragmented and scraped. What can I do?

"Ideally you want to avoid friction and washing," said Dr. Reeves. Of course I can't eliminate friction, but I can do something about washing off my scarce skin oils, and I can lubricate my skin.

I asked why my fingers crack right after I cut my nails. Dr. Reeves explained, "You might experience cracks close to the nail if you are using skin that technically belongs under the nail." This could certainly apply to me, since I love to have my nails very short. And apparently the problem is worse in winter because "cold, dry climates take water out of the skin and in the winter the heat in our houses dries out the air [and hence our skin] even more."

Also, as I get older, I notice that my skin seems to be getting drier. I wondered if that could be related to hormonal changes. "Skin does get drier after menopause," said Dr. Reeves. "It also coarsens in texture, which many people perceive as dryness. But older skin is dryer than young skin."

Some people swear by Superglue as a fix for finger cracks. But is it really safe, I wondered, to use on my skin? "Absolutely. One drop of it will not only ease the pain, after the alcohol [in it] stops stinging, but it aids healing by providing a protective layer for the skin." But let me give a warning: I once got Superglue on my skin by accident, and I developed blisters on my skin under the glue, and the skin in that area felt numb. Dr. Reeves told me this might be an allergic reaction, since one out of every two hundred to three hundred people is allergic to Superglue. (I'll stay with Nu Skin, that reliable drugstore product more than one *Strings* reader recommended.)

Next I asked Dr. Reeves if dry skin problems could be diet-related. "In extreme starvation cases the skin dries and cracks," he replied, "but the average American diet supplies enough minerals and vitamins for healthy skin."

I turned to nutritionist Susan Baum, a registered dietician in Fairfax, Virginia, for further advice on diet and skin health. Her answer: "If your dry skin problem is weather-related, then you don't have a nutritional deficiency. I have seen [dry skin due to vitamin or mineral deficiency] on rare occasions, but only in those persons who have an inborn error of metabolism, or those who suffer from out-and-out malnutrition."

According to Baum, people with such "inborn errors of metabolism" might not be able to utilize certain vitamins, but they would have chronic dermatitis, not just in winter. And the only people she has seen with malnutrition severe enough to cause dry skin are alcoholics who rarely eat. That excludes most of us!

So I returned to Dr. Reeves for advice on the best way to use lotion or cream to re-hydrate skin. He said that for maximum rehydration, you should "soak your hands in water (the cells soak up water), then immediately coat them in lotion, the heavier the better—like Vaseline. However," he admits, "this is too greasy to be practical for most people, particularly string players." So are there any creams he could recommend for a player like me? "Any heavy cream is good; light cream is less good but there is a new family of creams available, alpha-hydroxy acid lotions." The two acids found in these creams, lactic acid and glycolic acid, "provide a high-tech solution to your dry skin problem."

Feeling fully informed, I started thinking more carefully about my hands. There were a few key things I could do to help prevent cracks. The first was to give my hands an extra layer of protective skin over the layer that's already there: I needed gloves. I now use gloves to re-hydrate my skin after applying cream; to keep soaps, chemicals, food, and dust from taking the natural and man-made oils from my skin; and to keep my skin warm in cold weather. Of course you wear gloves to wash dishes and scrub sinks, right? I now wear "food service" gloves almost all the time when I'm in the kitchen, to avoid touching raw foods like peeled potatoes, apples, berries, and meats. The gloves are inexpensive (I get mine at the grocery store). I just have to remember to use them every time I handle food. It's easy to remember gloves when slicing onions or making meatballs, but do you think of putting them on to make a sandwich? You should, since basic ingredients like lunchmeat and pickles can spell trouble.

Here's another thing: did you ever notice how dry your hands feel after vacuuming? That's because you are rubbing dirt, an abrasive, into tiny cracks in your skin. Get out the gloves! Even something like chalk dust is drying, so when your three-year-old wants you to draw with chalk, put on your gloves first. And don't forget gloves for yard and garden work, particularly when the ground is cold and damp.

When my fingers get cold the skin feels somehow thinner and more brittle. That means I should carry a pair of gloves in any coat or jacket pocket at all times during the winter. If I walk to the corner to mail a letter, I'll put on gloves. If I get in the car and the steering wheel feels cold, I'll put on gloves. My rule of thumb is: if it's cold enough outside to wear a jacket, it's cold enough to wear gloves. I got some inexpensive bright-red chenille gloves on sale after Christmas last year, and their zaniness helps remind me to wear them.

I know this sounds burdensome at first, but you get used to it and so does your family (who might tease you at first about your regimen). I was absolutely religious about using gloves and lotions for three weeks before a recent recital, and I didn't get even one crack.

One final note: if you feel like your hands are suddenly drying out, especially during a rehearsal or concert, go ahead and put on some very light cream or lotion, even just a drop or two, right away: it can really make a big difference. (My personal favorite is Hawthorn Cream by the Body Shop. It soaks in quickly, doesn't feel greasy on the strings, makes my skin feel flexible, and comes in a conveniently tiny container.) Remember you want to avoid a crack, not treat one.

Alpha-hydroxy Lotions

According to Dr. Reeves, alpha-hydroxy lotions don't just put moisture on your skin; they "reach" your skin to produce another type of dead-skin layer that is more resistant to abrasion. They take two to four weeks to produce noticeable results. The creams can sting when you first apply them, due to tiny cracks under the skin, but that will go away after a few days. Dr. Reeves points out that these lotions will penetrate less well through the dead-skin layer on your hands (or feet), so you may need a stronger concentration of cream.

Over the counter, you can generally get creams that are five to eight percent lactic acid, one of the key ingredients of an alpha-hydroxy lotion. Some to look for are Lubriderm Moisture Recovery Cream (not the regular Lubriderm), which contains seven percent lactic acid, and the similar Eucerin Plus (again, not the regular Eucerin). LacHydrin 12 is a twelve percent cream that requires a prescription, but AmLactin is also twelve percent and can be obtained over the counter. It's possible to get fifteen, twenty, or even twenty-five percent glycolic-acid creams (the other key ingredient in these creams), but your physician must order them.

I went to my local beauty-supply store to see if I could find these creams easily. I did, as well as several other brands, such as Curel, that are also marketing alpha-hydroxy creams. I am buying a large bottle for regular winter use.

The best method of application, says Dr. Reeves, is to apply the cream and then wear disposable plastic gloves for three to six hours (or while you sleep) to help the cream penetrate your skin. "I don't recommend latex or rubber gloves for overnight use, since many people are allergic to them. But there is a huge market for vinyl examination gloves. You can buy them at beauty supply shops, paint stores, or even gas stations that supply gloves to customers to prevent gas smell on their hands." I found vinyl gloves easily at a local beauty supply store, a grocery store, and a paint store. They come in varying sizes but don't fit very well, so I prefer the more fitted "food service" gloves for keeping my skin protected. But I don't wear any gloves to bed; I prefer simply to rub on some thick cream and skip the gloves.

The idea that applying these creams for a few weeks can teach skin to behave differently is certainly intriguing, and I'm hoping for good results.

The source of true comfort is good body awareness and a well-practiced technique, supplemented by adjustments to one's instrument and surroundings.

-Tom Heimberg

Heimberg's Handy Hints: 8
Tips and Tricks
of the Trade

By Tom Heimberg

VIOLIST MICHAEL TREE has said, "Anything that improves the comfort of the musician improves the tone of the instrument." Playing a string instrument well and comfortably is a lifelong endeavor in which success can be measured in millimeters. Every little bit counts. That is why we string players are always seeking the most efficient fingering, the most gracefully appropriate bowing, the most productive way of practicing.

That is also why we put shoulder rests on our instruments and cushions on our chairs. Comfort can be sought everywhere, where the instrument touches the player and where the player touches the world. It has to do with the whole musician and the whole environment of music-making.

The basic source of true comfort is good body awareness and a well-practiced instrumental technique. That foundation can be supplemented, not replaced, by adjustments to one's instrument and surroundings. But once that foundation is in place (or under construction), there are many minor changes that can be made toward a freer enjoyment of playing.

I've been experimenting and adjusting for years, and not just with my instruments and the usual appurtenances (spare strings, shoulder pad, etc.). My viola case, like Batman's utility belt, also holds needle and thread, Velcro strips, cosmetic sponges, all-purpose rubber bands, scissors, surgical tubing, a length of bicycle inner tube, and more. I try things out. I putter. I tinker.

Here, then, are a few of my experimental results. I do not offer them as prescriptions, but as encouragements to make your own trials and adjustments. Doing so is part of our craft. It's part of the satisfaction, part of the comfort, and part of the fun.

Properly directing the bow is a little like being a parent; it requires a balance of firmness and permissiveness that takes years to learn. The contact points where our fingers touch the bow are among the most important places of our art. They are the transition areas between our intentions and our sound. The purposes of the mind, the weight of the arm, the subtleties of the fingers all focus at those spots. How we hold the bow influences everything else we do with the instrument.

I am very careful about how I describe holding the bow. I don't want the action to get burdened by heavy words. For example, I hate the expression "bow grip"—it sounds like something from the World Wrestling Federation. Instead, I think that words such as cradle, carry, or cherish give a better emotional sense of what bowing is like.

But sometimes, when there is a lot of playing to do, we have to cherish the bow for hours and hours at a time. At those times a little bit of help can be...a big help. One type of help is found by sliding something over the bowstick to make it a little larger and easier to hold. Some of the bowing aids I've seen used this way are three-inch lengths of surgical tubing, or the little rubber tubes sold in stationery stores as pencil grips, or small rubber plumbers' O-rings.

There's also what I'm using now: latex clerks' thimbles. You know, the rubber caps that you put over your thumb to help you turn pages of paper. I started trying this idea out when San Francisco Opera presented Wagner's *Ring* cycle last summer. It has really worked well for me, especially when playing tremolo during the fifth hour of *Götterdämmerung*. Just make a small hole in the thimble's tip (they come in several sizes—more room for experimenting), remove the frog from your bow, and slide the thimble on, with the large open end toward the tip of the bow. Work it on all the way up to the leather winding before replacing the frog. The result is a flexible bow helper whose stippled surface seems to be holding you as much as you're holding it. For added security it is also possible to add small holes that allow your third finger and thumb to touch the wood of the stick.

Another place of magic is where the instrument touches the player's body. This is significant for all string players, but especially for violinists and violists, who support their instruments against gravity. Shoulder rests or pads are a great aid.

I remember that in my student days there were still older violinists who referred to shoulder pads as "crutches," an insulting term that implied that anyone who used them was physically unfit to play the violin. This characterization was usually made by short men with broad shoulders and no necks (men "built like a fire hydrant," as violinist Stuart Canin once put it), who seemed to be able to "plug in" their violins and simply play. That doesn't work for everyone. Adjusting a shoulder rest to suit the body of the player is an important part of the search for comfort. Like most violists, I tinker a lot with my shoulder rest. Violas come in all shapes and sizes, violists come in all shapes and sizes, and the shapes and sizes of commercial shoulder rests are just as varied, but not always in the right way. So we use all kinds of tools to adjust them: cosmetic sponges, rubber bands and chamois, Velcro, handkerchiefs.

But often we also need to protect the instrument from the shoulder rest, to help our psychological comfort. Although I admire the ergonomic concepts of several commercial brands, I am alarmed by their engineering. There's too much hardware dangerously close to the wood of the instrument; any metal near the wood should have a protective covering. Bare wires can be covered with tubing. Vinyl tubing is strong and effective for straight wires, while surgical tubing is easier to bend around corners. Electricians' heat-shrink tube wrap is aesthetically pleasing once you've taken the time and effort to apply it. These can also be used on nuts, bolts, and similar protuberances.

Lately I have been using a simple device that covers the metal back of my shoulder rest: a piece of bicycle inner tube. Just get a used tube from the bicycle shop (they often will give them away), cut it to length, and slide it over the body of the shoulder rest, like a sleeve. It protects your instrument, provides a little extra padding, and sometimes even looks interesting.

Cellists may not need shoulder rests, but they have problems of their own. Ruth Land, an elegantly tall cellist in the San Francisco Opera Orchestra, wanted to sit straight when she played. But she had to bend her head to the right to avoid getting poked in the side of the head by the tuning peg on her C string. The solution: remove the peg and replace it with a gearing mechanism turned with a key. This adjustment works perfectly for her. She tells me that the product, Posture Peg, is quite popular among cellists in Los Angeles.

Here is another contribution to psychological comfort: taming the mute. All players need mutes, although we usually don't think much about them (unless they rattle, fall off in performance, or aren't there when the music says *con sordino*). But they are worth thinking about. During the great San Francisco Symphony tour of Europe and Russia in 1973, I was touched by the ingenuity of our Soviet colleagues. They did not have access to high quality manufactured mutes, but they had a practical alternative: money. They would tightly roll up a paper ruble note and thread it through the strings between the fingerboard and the bridge, where it could slide up and down as needed.

I thought that trick was an impoverished substitute for the real thing until twenty years later, when I saw some colleagues who had emigrated from the former Soviet Union. They were still using the same kind of technique, this time with dollars. I asked them about their money-mutes and got a compelling answer: "It does not fall off, it does not buzz, it works as mute, and it costs less than mute." Rolled up bills are easy enough to get, so I tried it with dollar bills and liked it. (Just think: you can use francs for French music, lire for Italian, Deutschmarks for German—very subtle musical effects!) More recently I've been trying thin strips of leather, or trim from old eyeglass cases, applied in the same way. With the right weight and firmness, the tone is sweet and the mute is silent when you slide it into place.

By the way, if you use a rubber mute and want to get rid of the creaky-squeaky sound it makes when you put it on or take it off the bridge in a hurry, try dripping a drop of candle paraffin into the slot and then wiping it off. According to violist Martin Anderson of the New Jersey Symphony, this provides just enough lubrication to eliminate the unwanted sound.

Going back to the theme of comfort, here is another important aid. In recent radio interviews, violinist Nadja Salerno-Sonnenberg has talked about having to "force calluses" after a layoff from playing. That's too bad. Forcing of any kind is not good for violin playing. There are other ways to firm up the left-hand fingertips–Nu Skin for example. This liquid bandage can be painted or sprayed onto the fingertip, and after just two minutes of drying the liquid forms a malleable protective cap for the finger. It can be played on immediately, while the finger re-establishes its own protective padding underneath. I've used the substance in a variety of circumstances: after layoffs, after washing in hot water, and even after cutting my finger in a kitchen accident. It worked well every time.

I'm sure every player has personal ideas for increasing creature comforts while playing–or for solving any of the little annoyances in a string player's life. Personally, I'm always looking for more.

A Helping Hand   9

TENSION-FREE BOWING TIPS THAT ADULT AMATEURS CAN GRASP

By James Reel

THE FIRST TIME a teacher hands us a string instrument, we figure the tricky part will be putting our left hand fingers in the correct spots to get the right notes. How hard can moving the bow with the right hand be?

Well, as we discover, the moment we first draw the bow across an open string, it's not that simple. Then, as we try to get a decent sound, a lot of us tighten up that right hand, use the wrong pressure in the wrong direction, and start making noises that remind us that strings used to be made of catgut.

Before we can produce the smooth sound that attracted us to strings in the first place, we have to overcome that tension in the bow hand. Florida freelance violinist and teacher Eden Vaning-Rosen has written an entire tome on the subject; it's called *The Violin Book 6a: Elements of a Tension-Free Bow Hand, with Etudes*.

She says that tension sets in when a muscle's natural motion gets halted in some way. And we aren't necessarily talking about anything as active as moving a bow or climbing stairs. As an experiment, Vaning-Rosen suggests that you sit with your feet flat on a hardwood or tile floor. Press your toes down against the floor, and hold them like this for a short while. "You'll not only feel your feet become tight," she points out, "but soon your calves, and then your thighs."

"What has happened? You created energy by your muscle motion against the floor. The energy could not travel freely into the hard floor, so the energy came back through the muscles following the same pathway along which it first traveled."

If you can do that to yourself just sitting there, you know you're in trouble if your bow hand is tense.

Right and Wrong

So how, exactly, does tension affect a violin bow hand? Here's Vaning-Rosen's explanation: "Think back to your first lessons, when you were learning to hold the bow correctly. At this point your hand was placed at the frog with the thumb under and the four fingers across the top. Right away you became aware, consciously or unconsciously, of a large strain on your pinky. The natural decision a student makes at this point is: "In order to hold this violin bow I'm going to have to hold it tightly with my pinky, because this bow is heavy!"

That's obvious if you're holding the bow in the air in front of you. The bow stick works like a long lever arm, and because of the pull of gravity, the longer a lever arm is, the heavier it feels. Your thumb under the frog acts as the lever's fulcrum, or support; your pinky literally gets the short end of the stick, supporting the actual weight of the bow, as well as the increased weight because of the length of the bow stick. Because of this, the pinky develops tension, which moves through the wrist and into the forearm.

But what happens when you place the bow down on the A string? Now the long bow is supported by the string, not your thumb, and your pinky can relax. You can even lift it up and down. Your whole hand is relaxed now, and you can focus on the front side of the hand, transferring any needed weight into the bow stick to achieve the sound you want.

"When a student doesn't realize that the feeling in the bow hand on the string is different from the feeling in the bow hand off the string, and thus continues to keep the tension in the hand after the bow is placed on the string," says Vaning-Rosen, "this continued tension in the pinky will equalize the weight being transferred into the other side. The bow therefore surfaces over the string, with little or no energy being transferred into the string. With little or no feeling of friction on the string, a strong, rich tone cannot be produced. A student should, therefore, be aware of how he starts each bow stroke, paying careful attention to any pinky tension."

She advocates consciously trying a technique the wrong way as well as the right way, so you can see and feel the difference. She suggests playing a line from an etude by Franz Wohlfahrt.

EXAMPLE 1: First, play this line and let your pinky remain tight after you place your bow on the string. Play it again, but when you place the bow, stop for a moment to relax the pinky and transfer weight to the front of the hand. Take a breath, then start the stroke. Notice the difference?

The first time through, let your pinky remain tight after you place your bow on the string. Listen to the sound you produce, and feel any tension in your hand.

Play through the example again, but this time, after placing your bow on the string, stop for a second to relax the pinky. Then transfer weight to the front side of the hand, becoming conscious of the natural cling (the weight of the bow and hand against the string). Take a deep breath, and then start the stroke. What was the difference in your bow sound?

"The motions of the bow strokes actually parallel the natural actions of body muscles," she says. "Body muscles alternate between contracting and relaxing in order to perform all the tasks demanded of them. Similarly, each different type of bow stroke is made up of a different set of tension and relaxation steps."

Try example 2, this time using a staccato bowing. Play through the line, keeping tension in your pinky. Notice the strained, unmusical sound of the stopped bow stroke.

EXAMPLE 2: Play through the line with a staccato bowing, keeping tension in your pinky. Play it again, releasing any pinky tension in your hand first.

Now play through the staccato line again, this time releasing any pinky tension in your hand first. Suggests Vaning-Rosen, "Press your first finger (using tension) on the bow before playing the staccato note, and release it immediately when the bow stroke starts, to get a good 'bell tone,' 'ka' sound. Continue to press and relax for each staccato note."

"It's essential to identify and remove any negative tension from your hand to master the different bowing skills. Excess tension in the hand can even cause a bow to bounce when you start a legato stroke. Try as much as possible to not lift the bow off the string. Make sure after any small lift of the bow that you do not tense up your hand when your bow returns to the string."

"Once the initial awareness of removing unwanted tensions from the hand is accomplished," Vaning-Rosen continues, "the next level of training involves achieving springlike bow-hand motions. Ivan Galamian, in his book *The Principles of Violin Playing and Teaching*, describes the action and the function of bow-arm technique as 'based on a system of springs.' (Spring-like motion is essentially gathering energy into an object and then releasing it.) In order for the body's natural springs to work, the muscles and joint must be flexible."

Vaning-Rosen advocates this basic exercise to demonstrate the springlike motions of the bow hand: Place your bow hand in the air in front of you and make a fist, bending back your fingers and your wrist.

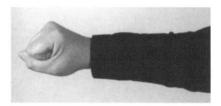

FIGURE 1: (a) Hold your bow hand in the air in front of you and make a fist, bending back your fingers and wrist.

Then relax your hand, straightening your fingers.

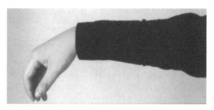

FIGURE 1: (b) Relax your hand, straightening your fingers.

That's not what most people mean by the term "hand-spring" but it does show you the natural springing motions of your hand, and, in its relaxed state, your hand is in a prime position for grasping the bow.

Understanding this concept of tension, relaxation, and flexibility is the hard part. Once you've got it, you can start a progression of drills like those in Vaning-Rosen's book—with which, in her words, "any student can master smooth bow changes and a plethora of more advanced strokes."

"Great artists appear to play effortlessly, with their music just pouring forth," she adds. "Achieving this effortlessness starts with the bow arm's ability to control tension and use relaxation, thus allowing the natural energy of the body's motions to carry one's music forth."

When it comes to a musician's hands, small problems can quickly become big problems.

-David Templeton

Finger Tips 10

By David Templeton

"WHEN IT COMES to protecting one's hands and fingers, violinists are pretty careful," observes Dr. Robert Markison. "Generally," he adds, "violinists are not getting cut doing dishes." True enough. When was the last time anyone heard of a violinist absentmindedly lopping off a forefinger with a soapy steak knife? Still, as Markison has observed first- ... uh... hand, accidents do happen.

Even the most conscientious players can injure themselves now and then. While one can take precautions against accidents, some players in the course of their careers will develop tendinitis or carpal tunnel syndrome, fracture or crush a finger or fingers, or even sever the *flexor digitorum profundus.*

Fortunately, experts like Markison can help. A broadly trained physician and hand surgeon, Markison is an associate clinical professor of surgery at the University of California at San Francisco Medical School. He was a co-founder, in 1984, of a ground-breaking health program for performing artists at UCSF, and served as head of hand surgery at San Francisco General Hospital's trauma center through the 1980s. During that time he treated, in his words, "large-print editions of misery," which included severed hands reattached with the aid of a microscope, and "small-print editions of misery," of which the most common were cumulative trauma and repetitive strain.

With such experience, Markison, also a widely recorded woodwind musician and composer, has become a worldwide authority on the care, repair, and injury prevention of the musical hand. Says Markison, "I want to see to it that people don't suffer unduly as they try to measure out time gracefully in music."

Small Problem, Big Pain

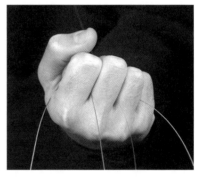

Carpal tunnel syndrome and various forms of tendinitis are perhaps the most common injuries suffered by string players. "Some people are prone, by DNA family history, to arthritis, and others have the bad luck of too much playing, too much practice," he explains. That said, Markison warns that there are more serious conditions that can masquerade as carpal tunnel syndrome or tendinitis.

"What you have to be aware of," he says, "is that sometimes a person will be told they have carpal tunnel syndrome when in fact they'll have a cervical spine problem at C5 or C6, which is masquerading as carpal tunnel because the thumb and index are numb. Neck and thorax problems can be masqueraders," says Markison, "and hand surgeons, hand specialists, and physicians in general are at their worst when they assume, *a priori*, that it's only a hand problem, because a hand doesn't live an isolated life."

When it comes to a musician's hands, small problems can quickly become big problems. There is no better example of this than the issue of cracked fingertips. *Neurodermatitis* is the medical term for it: itchy, cracking, raw broken skin, all for no apparent reason. Such a condition, of course, is not helped by what Lori Stotko, San Francisco-area certified hand therapist (CHT) and a musician for thirty-eight years, calls "persistently irritating activity such as scratching or pressing strings."

With such a condition, there is usually an element of nerve damage, hence the *neuro* prefix, and there is always a heightened possibility of developing a skin fungus. The skin becomes abraded by the strings, says Stotko, and then a fungus can set in. While most string players form calluses, others just don't, the fingertips become dried and cracked, but never heal.

It is believed that warm soapy water can exacerbate the problem (a good excuse to have someone else wash the dishes), and in many cases, the condition grows worse in midwinter, most likely in response to drier weather. Some musicians use a humidifier in the house and drink an extra glass or two of water each day during the dry-weather season.

Many dermatologists recommend that players with this condition use "finger cots" or "finger cones" while playing. These are the thin latex gloves commonly used to keep moisture or dirt out of cuts and abrasions and fresh stitches. The fingertips can also be treated with a cortisone ointment or triple-antibiotic cream. Usually, neurodermatitis responds slowly to cortisone cream, while your basic dry fingers respond better to petroleum jelly and triple-antibiotic cream. Fungus, of course, can be eliminated only with the use of an antifungal cream.

To determine which course of treatment to use, always see a dermatologist first. As in many other finger-related injuries, seek treatment as early as possible to counter the risk of further skin damage.

When to Take a Break

What happens, though, when you do sustain an injury of some kind, yet you have a full rehearsal calendar or touring schedule? When is an injury so worrisome that a musician should take a break from playing? In the world of professional music, many players end up making hard choices whenever they encounter physical injuries.

"I tend to play through injuries," says Sara Sant'Ambrogio, cellist with the New York-based Eroica Trio. "I've played with a broken elbow. I broke my elbow on my left arm ten years ago in a car accident, and I've played with a fractured finger."

The finger incident occurred early last year, while on tour with Eroica, and just before entering a studio to record a Beethoven CD with the Prague Chamber Orchestra. While no one would have blamed Sant'Ambrogio for canceling the rest of the tour and postponing the studio sessions, she chose to soldier on and play with the damaged digit. "My finger was five times the size it was supposed to be," she recalls. "I don't know how I made it. The power of the mind is a heck of a lot stronger than we give it credit for. There was never a question in my mind. I never allowed it. I determined to do my best, and that my best was going to be good enough."

Now that her hand is fully mended, Sant'Ambrogio says that the experience provided a significant opportunity to learn and grow as a player. "It's made me a much better cellist," she says, "because I had to completely dissect how I hit things, how I do things. I had to look at what parts of my body I was using when I play."

After hearing Sant'Ambrogio's story, one has to wonder how common such occurrences are in the musical world. How often does a musician break or hurt a finger and continue playing while injured? And is this a good idea—or a very, very bad one?

"It happens," says Markison. "It's not the end of the world. Sometimes a musician has to do something like that. It's not great, but it can be OK as long as you have the safety net of a specialist who can follow you along and be sensitive to the needs of music. The hand can be pretty unforgiving. Any fracture that's set in the hand of a musician needs to be set very well."

Stotko represents those professionals who discourage players from ever playing "through the pain." That said, she recommends that players approach their healing process the way athletes do. "The musician should continue playing in a safe, modified fashion to maintain dexterity, motor patterns, and to keep the tendons and ligaments in shape for playing music, while doing a lot of stretching before and after playing—stretching is the key—but to always be slow and gentle."

For most tendon injuries, Stotko says her typical treatment plan involves fifteen or twenty minutes of practice, followed by rest periods of five to twenty minutes, depending on the acuteness of the injury.

As for Sant'Ambrogio's assertion that by playing though her injury she has become a better player, Markison says he's observed such things plenty of times.

"You wait for adversity to push you into something that should have been normal routine," he says. "But hopefully, most musicians can work by prevention, and learn from that, rather than wait to fall into unnecessary patches of misery."

Three Things to Think About

How does one avoid injury, and what should be done when injuries occur? Here are some healthful hints for full-time or part-time players.

1. "Don't clamp down." According to Dr. Markison, it is very important to think and rethink chin and shoulder rests so you are not clamping down as you play. "If you do clamp down," he says, "you're going to have a web of muscle tightening around the nerves, which will have an adverse impact all the way to the fingertips."

2. Maintain good posture, which can mean everything including your hands and fingers. "Straighten up and fly right," says Markison, "in order to avoid injuries."

3. For players recovering from tendinitis, Markison recommends taking several actions. These include rethinking your practice schedule, taking more breaks, drinking plenty of water to keep your system well-hydrated and, ultimately, your joints well-lubricated, and making sure that your hands are warm whenever you play. "You don't want to ever play cold-handed," he says, "Because blood flow matters greatly. Cool-handed string players are at far greater risk than warm-handed players.

Pain is never gain.

-Ruth F. Brin

Playing Hurt

11

DOCTORS, MUSICIANS, AND TEACHERS TALK ABOUT WHEN TO STOP, WHAT TO DO, HOW TO COPE

By Ruth F. Brin

MUSICIANS ARE ATHLETES, but they play for a whole lifetime, not just a peak period in youth. Your brain isn't all in your head. The easy way to play is the best way. Pain is never gain. It is time for musicians to come out of the closet and admit when playing hurts, and for a majority of students and professionals it does hurt.

These are among the many striking points brought out at the Second Annual Conference on the Identification, Prevention, and Treatment of the Medical Problems of Musicians, held at the University of Minnesota, April 14-16, 1989.

Janet Horvath—the petite, surprisingly young assistant principal cellist of the Minnesota Orchestra—made her BBC debut recently, and is a frequent soloist. While a student of Janos Starker at Indiana University, she had tendinitis, and was terrified that she would have to abandon her chosen career. Starker insisted she rest, although highly competitive students are afraid to stop practicing. He found medical help for her, and eventually she was able to resume her schedule. She developed an interest in the medical problems of musicians and sparked the first Playing Hurt Conference, bringing together doctors and musicians for the first time. She was a major planner of the 1989 conference, and presented a carefully made list of ways to prevent overuse injuries at the end of the conference. She says telling students "no pain, no gain" is both false and misleading.

The Minnesota meetings have been the only ones to involve both musicians and health professionals, an exciting combination. In 1989, more than two hundred participated: doctors, physical therapists, nurses, and other caregivers; pop, jazz, and classical musicians, among them students, amateurs, and professionals; and, encouragingly, a few orchestra administrators. Conferees came from nine states and Canada, while the staff was international. Kato Havas, the charming British violin teacher who started out as a Hungarian child

Janet Horvath, principal organizer of the series of Playing Hurt Conferences, is assistant principal cellist of the Minnesota Orchestra.

prodigy and now teaches all over the world, was a keynoter. Another famous teacher, pianist Dorothy Taubman, teaches in New York and Massachusetts. Both are known for helping professionals overcome painful playing habits. Arnold Jacobs, retired principal tuba of the Chicago Symphony, is an authority that spoke on the relationship of physical to motivational aspects of playing. Doctors included Alice Brandfonbrener, who is a founder of the young branch of performing arts medicine. She edits a journal (*Medical Problems of Performing Artists*), directs the clinic for performing artists at Northwestern Memorial Hospital in Chicago, and for some years co-directed the Aspen summer meetings, for doctors only, in this field.

A friendly atmosphere and a sense of discovery prevailed, as doctors—nearly all musicians themselves—presented their slide talks (always with a cartoon to precede the boring anatomical diagrams), and music teachers demonstrated new techniques and ideas. What follows is a report on the highlights. Needless to say, the descriptions of injuries you find here shouldn't be construed as diagnoses based on the information you find in this article. But there is much that you can learn about potentially damaging practices, and a great deal of food for thought about your own habits and experiences, in the material presented at the Playing Hurt Conference.

The immediate cause of injury in a musician can be as basic as simply choosing the wrong instrument, or switching to an unfamiliar one. Some argue, for example, that a small person should probably not try to be a professional string bass player. Doctors speak about strength, conditioning, build, size, and diseases such as arthritis or other structural or postural abnormalities. Music teachers like Havas and Taubman, on the other hand, emphasized that with correct technique and motivation, a person with a small hand or other physical limitations can play Chopin on the piano and Brahms on the violin.

Faulty technique can clearly play a major role in causing injury. Several doctors agreed that about half of patients experienced injury when making a sudden increase in practice time or other major change. For example, switching to a new repertoire, a new teacher, or a different instrument (such as from modern cello to baroque cello) are often times when injury occurs. Changes in other activities, such as recreation or job, can have unforeseen consequences. No musician can call new muscle groups into service, or use them in new ways, and expect them to function as well as those developed over a period of years. All of these occurrences are lumped under the heading "overuse."

Clearly, musicians must be in good health and follow a routine of general (in addition to musical) exercise, get regular rest, and pay attention to pain and discomfort when playing. Over and over again, overuse emerged as the major cause for medical problems. Hours of practice and play must be controlled; rest from play, ideally one day a week (don't even touch your instrument!), is essential.

For many, the idea of rest was revolutionary. The manager of a Canadian baroque ensemble, convinced that musicians must practice daily to maintain technique, evinced surprise that so many of the musicians on a nonstop two-week tour complained of general illness (colds and flu) and tendinitis. She laughed about this experience, but some of her musicians were probably crying. Orchestra managers clearly must hear the message of prevention from medical and musical personnel.

Neurologist Richard Lerdeman, director of the Cleveland Clinic for Performing Arts, who was introduced as the father of this branch of medicine, defined tendinitis as a "repetition strain injury" resulting from overuse, that may involve muscle, tendon, joint ligament, joint tissue (such as the bursa), or nerves—in other words, any of the soft tissue of the body, and for musicians, most often the hand, arm, shoulder, neck, and back, roughly in that order.

Overuse tendinitis has various forms, many recognized by doctors more than a century ago. Among them are housemaid's knee, writer's cramp, gamekeeper's thumb (renamed in honor of the oboe as oboist's thumb), weaver's bottom, and manure shoveler's hip (he who shovels manure turns away from the stink and twists his hip until it hurts).

"Writer's cramp" (its medical name is focal distonia) may affect musicians as well as keypunch operators and typists in greater proportion than the general public. It was first observed in scribes writing by hand. Not only is pain involved but also a loss of control of the motions of the fingers. No totally successful treatment is known, but help is available.

"Fiddler's shoulder" has been added to the list. The rotator cuff consists of four muscles that hold the arm bone (humerus) to the shoulder bone. These two bones fit loosely, unlike the hip, which is a ball and socket joint in a comparatively rigid arrangement. In the shoulder, the bones merely touch, held by these muscles, and thus move with greater freedom than the hip. But, as many violinists and violists have discovered in overusing the bow arm, the joint is relatively weak. Cellists may also strain the rotator cuff muscles when they move the arm away from the side of the body. Pain may occur with use, or on raising and lowering the arm.

Hand pain is frequent in string players who are "double jointed" or have what doctors call "joint laxity" or "benign laxity." Inappropriate bow holds may be hard on thumbs. As musicians know, the third and fourth fingers are the most vulnerable, and double stops the most likely to precipitate problems. More women than men seem to succumb to this type of pain.

Carpal tunnel syndrome occurs when pressure on the nerves in the carpal tunnel, which runs through the wrist, cause numbness, prickling, or loss of control in the hand or fingers. Treatments include rest, icing, cortisone or other injections, and surgery as a last resort.

Although little research has been funded in music medicine, a few surveys have indicated remarkably high percentages of musicians who suffer from pain while playing. For example, a Cleveland clinic survey showed fifty-eight percent of students at a conservatory, thirty percent of professionals, and eleven percent of teachers with "pain problems." In 1986, the Fry Survey of professional symphony players showed sixty-four percent complaining. A different survey of full-time orchestras yielded a figure of seventy-eight percent!

Many violinists and violists suffer from a jaw problem, TMJ, or pain in the temporal mandibular joint, associated with anxiety. A well-informed dentist should be able to help. Changes in bite because of other dental work like crowns or artificial teeth are more likely to affect wind players.

Hearing loss may occur not only from playing in a rock band but also from playing in a symphony orchestra, particularly in front of the brasses or percussion. Once lost, hearing cannot be restored, although hearing aids may help. Prevention includes not practicing in a room full of hard surfaces, and especially wearing earplugs during exposure to loud noise. The Minnesota Orchestra has furnished clear plexiglass shields on the backs of chairs for those players directly in front of the brasses. Piccolo players are advised to practice on the flute. Carry earplugs and use them when the noise seems too heavy. Musicians should avoid noisy hobbies, such as metal working or hunting. If you are concerned about your hearing, you should have an audiogram to establish a base line. Small changes will show up in future tests, in time to warn you to take preventative measures.

There was a brief but helpful talk on AIDS by a family practitioner, Daniel Bowers, who is also a vocalist. He made it clear that musicians should not worry about contact with saliva, which sometimes is sprayed out by singers or dumped by horn players. There is no documented case of salivary transmission. The AIDS virus dies quickly on exposure to air, even in blood or any other body fluid. Sweat does not transmit AIDS. It is safe to use the same bathroom as an AIDS patient. He suggests that if any bodily fluid is spilled or discharged, the person who cleans up should wear rubber gloves and use a solution of one part bleach to ten parts water. A student and teacher can safely share mouthpieces (wind players). Finally, for the AIDS victim who may be your friend or fellow worker, it is very important for you, the healthy artist, to offer warm support. A touch on the shoulder, a hug, a kiss (even on the mouth) are all safe for you and important to keep your friend encouraged and functioning.

Stage fright may be the most common problem for a performer—and it is the quicker, more energetic, brighter performer who is more apt to suffer. This news should be of some comfort to sufferers! When tremor or stiffening occurs, beta-blockers in small doses before performance are the most often prescribed drug. Use under doctor's advice! Doctors may also prescribe tranquilizers or sedatives, which must be used with care because they may affect coordination. Deep or long psychoanalytical treatment is very seldom indicated, but sometimes short sessions of psychotherapy or counseling may be helpful. The sensitivity and motivation of the therapist are important, and the musician will be able to sense this. A psychiatrist pointed out that musicians who spend long hours alone practicing may become lonely, isolated individuals who need to make some effort to have a satisfactory social life.

Alexander Technique for relaxation and improved posture was presented at the conference, and other techniques such as massage of various kinds and Feldenkrais therapy were also discussed briefly.

Kato Havas spoke about the musician concentrating on giving music to the audience, rather than thinking about his or her fears of making mistakes. (Rubinstein would choose one beautiful woman in his audience and play to her.) Focus and concentration will often allay fears. Confidence in technique also helps the nervous artist. Enjoying what you are doing—making music for others—is key to good performance and confident playing.

When it comes to tendinitis, the treatment options are equally various. The musician with mild and occasional pain should treat herself or himself with rest or with short periods of icing the painful spot alternated with rest. If the malady lingers, it is time to take the problem to a teacher, coach, doctor, or therapist. Patience is essential. Healing takes time and rest is often the best medicine, even after consultation.

Other solutions include oral medications such as anti-inflammatories, muscle relaxants, or painkillers; cortisone injections; splints, braces, or other types of support; and finally, surgery. However, surgery should always be a last resort, because scar tissue is inevitable and may interfere with maximum motion.

A neurologist, Dr. Frank Wilson, highlighted one reason to avoid surgery with a fascinating theory: "An operation on your hand is an operation on your brain." The brain—the "place" for thinking, remembering, and controlling the muscles—is not in the head but in the entire central nervous system, from the head through the spinal column and in all the nerves going out to the rest of the body, including the hand and fingers. Most musicians have had the experience of letting their hands play a piece of music without conscious direction. The doctor says that indeed the memory is at least partially in the hands. (This is also an argument for practicing slowly enough so you don't practice mistakes and thus teach them to your hands!)

If you go to a physician, find one who is a musician and understands your problems. If possible, locate a performing arts clinic. The doctor should be willing to watch you play your instrument in order to see what is causing the strain and pain. The same is true if you go directly for some kind of physical therapy. Physical therapy, Alexander Technique, Feldenkrais, other types of prescribed exercise, massage, ice, and heat all may have a place in your treatment, whether for relaxation before going onstage, for relief of pain, or for easier position while playing.

If you go to a coach or teacher, you should get help in finding more appropriate ways to stand, sit, and hold and play your instrument. The watchwords here seem to be: *things that feel right sound right* or *the easy way to play is the best way*. For example, violinists and violists should have a combination of chin rest (perhaps custom made) and shoulder rest that allow the head to remain centered and the neck to be in a normal position, not twisted or bent. The instrument should fit comfortably so that it is not necessary to grip with the chin. Often this means holding the instrument lower than the musician is accustomed to. All string players should sit in such a way that they can stand up without shifting their weight—it should already be forward, partially on the feet.

Whether specialists in piano, strings, or winds, teachers at the conference emphasized that *you play with your whole body—your back, your shoulders, your arm, your hand—not just with your fingers*. Getting off-center, whether in the spine or twisting the hand or any other part of the body, is to be avoided. Play from a balanced position, again whether of hand and arm or of the whole body. Musicians should also find ways to balance the instrument they are holding to put the least weight on their own muscles. Violinists should particularly avoid hunching over their instruments. Although teachers spoke at length about balance and symmetry, this must be worked out for each individual, so that here only the general principles can be mentioned.

Ergonomics, the science of making adaptive equipment for people with special needs or special jobs, may be a boon to performers. Humans weren't really designed to walk on two feet, use complex tools, or play the violin. However, some doctors are now ingeniously developing equipment to help musicians. Examples include a wedge-shaped cushion, thicker at the back of the chair, to improve seating for string players, or a slightly bent flute to keep the player from bending her neck. There is even a harness developed in Australia that totally holds a violin, so the player need not use chin or arm at all for holding. Custom-molded chin rests can be had as well.

Cellists might want to order a "dycen" from an occupational therapy catalogue. This mushy looking disc was developed to hold plates to the table for patients with only one arm, but it will do a fine job of sticking to the floor and holding your endpin in place.

Dr. Richard Norris, an ingenious and enthusiastic young man who teaches at the New England Conservatory of Music, made these suggestions, and a good many more about carrying your instrument. Cello and bass players should have wheels on the bottoms of their cases. He urges devising straps for your fiddle that allow you to carry it like a backpack. This will keep your posture straight instead of bending you out of shape when you carry the weight on one side. Cello endpins can be modified for individual players. In general, it was noted that modern instruments are somewhat easier to play than their baroque versions, and that with some conscious effort instruments may be modified further to make them easier to play.

Many suggestions for prevention are inherent in the discussion of musicians' problems and treatments, but a few additional ones were bought out, especially by Janet Horvath, the young cellist who stimulated the development of this conference.

Musicians should pay attention to their general health, remembering that they are lifelong athletes. Regular rest, exercise, and good diet are all important. Musicians should sit and walk with excellent posture.

A number of pointers were mentioned for practice. Warm up slowly. Hands may be dipped in warm—not hot—water during cold weather. Take a five- or ten-minute break for every hour of practice: get up, move around, breathe deeply. Take a day off from practice once a week.

Many speakers mentioned practicing away from the instrument, or imaging, although no detailed description was given. You can imagine yourself playing the piece through as an aid to memorization. Do it while you're riding in a bus or train but not when you're driving a car!

Sports are fine: enjoy yourself, but please, no volleyball or karate. Try not to overemphasize the importance of one competition or audition; set your own standards, prepare well, and remember you will have other opportunities. Be alert when changing practice habits; when encountering a new teacher, new repertoire, or a new instrument; when increasing your practice time; or when playing in a cold room (watch out for churches!): all are factors in "overuse." Have a sensible attitude toward pain. Tolerate some minor pain occasionally, but if it persists and a day off doesn't work, look for some good professional help.

Some people are probably more prone to overuse injuries, just as some are less resistant to colds.

-Richard Norris, M.D.

Overuse Injuries 12

HOW STRING PLAYERS CAN RECOGNIZE, PREVENT, AND TREAT THEM

By Richard Norris, M.D.

OVERUSE INJURIES ARE, unfortunately, all too common among instrumentalists. But the good news is that they are largely preventable. And when they do occur, most can be treated through a combination of proper care and a change in the habits or activities that caused them. All musicians, from casual players to seasoned professionals, should learn the causes of overuse injuries in order to prevent their occurrence, and the signs of such injuries so as to recognize them at the earliest possible time.

First, what is an overuse injury? The condition occurs when any biological tissue, muscle, bone, tendon, ligament, etc., is stressed beyond its physical limit. This results in micro trauma to the body part; microscopic tears that lead to small amounts of bleeding and swelling within the injured area. For instance, runners and dancers frequently sustain stress or fatigue fractures, but musicians more commonly develop "tendinitis." The reason I put the word in quotes is that often the painful part is not the tendon itself, but the muscle attached to the tendon. However, since the word tendinitis is so familiar to musicians, we'll use it with the understanding that it refers to the muscle-tendon unit.

Overuse injuries are classified as acute or chronic. The acute overuse injury occurs when a musician learns a new phrase or trill and is determined to master it before going to bed that evening. He practices it over and over again for three or four hours, and the next day his hand or arm is stiff and painful. The chronic overuse injury takes place more insidiously over a longer period of time. Such is the tendinitis that is first evidenced as a very mild discomfort, and over the course of weeks or months becomes progressively severe.

Predisposing Factors

There are at least ten general factors that predispose a musician to suffer from overuse injuries:

Richard Norris, M.D.

1. **Genetic predisposition.** Some people are probably more prone to overuse injuries, just as some are less resistant to colds. Statistically, young women seem most at risk for overuse injuries. The reasons are not clear, but perhaps since women are more likely to seek health care than men, they are disproportionately represented in the statistics. Or perhaps because women's muscles are smaller, they are more susceptible to damage.

2. **Inadequate physical conditioning.** Muscles that are tight, weak, and inadequately stretched and exercised are more susceptible to overuse injuries than muscles that are strong and flexible. This raises the separate topic of physical conditioning for musicians.

Physical education in music schools and conservatories has been sorely neglected. Awareness of the importance of physical conditioning and exercise for musicians should increase.

3. **Sudden or abrupt increase in the amount of playing time.** This is perhaps the most common cause of overuse injuries. They often occur during summer music camps where a student who has been playing three to four hours per day suddenly starts to play seven to eight hours per day.

4. **Errors of technique.** One of the most common technical errors is playing with excessive tension, which causes the muscles to work extra hard. This is particularly common in string players' left hands when bowing *forte*. Despite the increase in pressure at the bow, the left hand should not have to press down much harder than when playing *piano*. Often the player is not aware of this. Pressing down even twenty to thirty percent harder than necessary on the strings may have a cumulative effect, and result in a gradual progressive overuse injury. In fact, tendinitis in the left forearm, particularly of the extensor muscles (the back of the forearm) is the commonest injury I see among violinists and violists in my practice.

Problems with excessive tension in muscle force also occur in the neck and left shoulder area in fiddlers. This is often due to inadequate or improperly fitted chin and shoulder rests. An excessively high elbow on the bowing arm will lead to a predisposition toward right shoulder problems, as the tendons in the right shoulder get impinged between the arm bone and the shoulder bone. Cellists have the same problem if they don't rotate the cello slightly toward the right arm to facilitate bowing on the upper strings. Modern scientific techniques such as motion analysis, which has been used to evaluate the technique of professional and Olympic athletes, may also become widely available in the musical field to give us a better understanding of bowing and fingering techniques. This is already happening in some centers, along with studies of the muscles involved in such actions as vibrato.

5. **Change in instrument.** Switching from violin to viola, from one size viola to another, or to an instrument that has a different bridge height can all cause overuse injuries. Whenever there is a change in instrument, the musician should back off slightly from his practice schedule and build up again over the course of a week or two. The same is true when changing repertoire or teacher.

6. **Errors in practice habits.** I feel that musicians should learn to regard playing their instruments as physical activity. When asked about warm-up habits, people often report that they don't warm up at all, or consider simply playing scales or a few slow pieces as enough of a warm-up. One plays a musical instrument with the entire body. A good warm-up that includes the neck, arms, shoulders, upper and lower back, at the very least, is important to prevent overuse injuries. Exercises might include slow rolling of the head, (both clockwise and counterclockwise), slow shoulder shrugs and rolls, side bends, and torso twists. In general, practice sessions should be limited to about forty-five minutes, with no less than a five-

minute break to relax and shake out muscles. (One may continue to practice for several hours in this fashion.) Difficult passages or those that require awkward fingering should be practiced in small, short segments of not more than five minutes each. Go back and practice something else and then return to the difficult segment. This will help avoid overuse injuries.

7. **Inadequate rehabilitation of previous injuries.** This factor is often overlooked. The tendinitis, muscle sprain, back or neck problem that has been treated just enough so that the person is able to resume playing, but that is not completely resolved, is likely to flare up over and over again with any additional stress. It is important to pursue therapy until the player is completely free of pain and has full range of motion, and endurance, strength, and coordination return.

8. **Improper body mechanics and posture.** This is where disciplines such as yoga and Alexander Technique are so important. A slumped posture and other poor body mechanics increase the risk for injury, particularly neck and back problems. This also applies to carrying instruments. Of course, the heavier the instrument, the more problems it presents, especially for a smaller person. In general, don't carry a heavy instrument with only one hand or hang it from one shoulder, as this creates undue strain on the shoulder and back. Instead, get a strap that is long enough to go over the head and across the chest. This distributes the weight of the instrument evenly. (Altieri in Denver, makes a variety of string cases with backpack attachments.) For heavier instruments there are backpack-type sacks or gig bags available.

For even larger instruments such as cello and bass, use wheels on the bottom of the case when feasible. Observe proper body mechanics—such as bending from the knees, and keeping loads close to the body—when lifting and carrying heavier string instruments.

9. **Stressful non-musical activities.** Refinishing furniture, pulling weeds, typing, knitting, or needle-work can all result in tendinitis-like problems. As with playing an instrument, these injuries can be avoided by awareness, frequent rests, and moderation in duration and intensity of the activity.

10. **Anatomical variation.** String players may experience problems resulting from anatomical anomalies and exacerbated by the demands of a particular instrument. Examples are thoracic outlet syndrome (nerve or blood vessel compression at the base of the neck from an extra cervical rib), increased joint laxity, or abnormal tendon connections or insertions.

Symptoms

How do you know if you have developed an overuse injury? The most common indicator is pain or discomfort. Overuse injuries are graded into five categories:

1. Pain at one site only, and pain that stops when playing stops.

2. Pain at multiple sites.

3. Pain that persists well beyond the time when the musician stops playing, along with some loss of coordination.

4. All the above. In addition, many activities of daily living (ADLs) begin to cause pain.

5. All the above, but *all* daily activities that engage the affected body part cause pain.

Most overuse injuries fall into categories 1, 2, or 3. The earlier the symptoms are recognized and treated, the sooner and more completely recovery occurs. Be aware that in the earliest stages, overuse injuries may feel like stiffness without significant amounts of pain.

Nerve Compression

Numbness and tingling, the feeling of pins and needles, or electric shock-type sensations are usually indicative of nerve compression. This occurs most commonly at the wrist and is called carpal tunnel syndrome (CTS), which usually causes numbness and tingling in the thumb, and index and middle fingers. CTS can be associated with a flexed wrist position, for instance as when playing in tenth position or above on the violin or viola. Here the wrist is extremely flexed, particularly on the viola. Avoid irritating the nerve at the wrist by practicing in the higher position only for short periods of time, if possible.

If the nerve compression occurs at the elbow, it is called cubital tunnel syndrome. The ulnar nerve that lies in the groove on the inside of the elbow (the so-called "funny bone") is compressed, and when the elbow is bent (flexed) the canal or cubital tunnel narrows and the nerve is stretched at the same time. The left arm of the cellist when playing in the first position, and of the violinist and violist when playing in higher positions is particularly vulnerable. One possible reason for increased risk in string players is that the muscles that press the fingers down onto the fingerboard, and bring the wrist into position to play in the higher positions on violin or viola, surround the ulnar nerve at the elbow. When these muscles are working and contracting, they cause increased compression on the nerve in this area. Symptoms of cubital tunnel syndrome are not only pain in the elbow region, but numbness and tingling in the fourth and fifth fingers, where the ulnar nerve ends, and loss of coordination. Nerves can also be compressed in the neck, producing similar symptoms in the hand. Electro diagnosis testing (electromyography, or EMG) can help pinpoint the sources of nerve compression problems.

Treatment

Perhaps the most important treatment is rest. We all know how difficult it is for professional musicians to take time off to rest, so we must borrow the concept of relative rest from sports medicine. This may mean cutting back on practice and performance rather than stopping completely. Of course, whether or not one must do this depends on the severity of the injury. For students there is less justification for not markedly cutting back or stopping playing for a brief period of time when necessary. It is better to postpone a jury or an audition than to play badly because of an injury. During the period of relative rest, technique should be assessed by a professional, looking especially for areas of excessive tension or stress. If these are deemed significant factors by either the teacher or the physician, consider a stress management program that includes biofeedback training. Biofeedback can be used for both general muscle relaxation and while playing the instrument, so you can learn to relax the specific muscle groups that may be overworking. Alexander lessons may also be helpful.

Easy stretching exercises are also important to maintain length and movement in injured muscles and tendons. These should be preceded by gentle warmth to help relax the affected part. Stretching should be done only to the point of mild discomfort. As pain from the injury subsides, institute gentle strengthening exercises. This is best done under the supervision of an occupational or physical therapist, but may be continued at home if you are very judicious. Remember that the muscles being strengthened are small, and it is better to proceed slowly and with caution than to risk re-injury. With forearm muscle tendinitis, pay special attention to strengthening the upper arms, chest, and trunk.

Thermo therapy in the form of ice, massage, and gentle heat is often effective. Heat should be applied before stretching and strengthening, with ice used afterward for five to ten minutes. Ice, rather than heat, should be used in acutely inflamed (hot) conditions. Anti-inflammatory medications such as Motrin, aspirin, Indocin, and others may be used, but should never be the primary treatment. If there is a history of bleeding tendencies or stomach ulcers, be especially cautious when using these medications.

Activities of Daily Living

One of the most commonly overlooked reasons for treatment failure in what might appear to be an adequate treatment program is ignoring the effects of activities of daily living (ADLs). When musicians complain of pain that accompanies ordinary activities such as brushing hair or teeth, opening doorknobs and the like, coupled with inability to play for a number of weeks, I always refer them for a session or two with the occupational therapist. During these sessions, ADLs are evaluated and modified, and adaptive equipment is introduced if necessary. There are many adaptive devices developed to help people with severe arthritis that make ADLs easier on the arms and hand. These devices include built-up foam handles for eating utensils, writing utensils, hairbrushes, and razors. Levers attached to doorknobs ease opening. Jar wrenches remove lids without force, key holders prevent pinching the key between thumb and index finger when opening doors.

Driving can be very hard on the arms, particularly in a car without power steering or automatic shift. Drive as little as possible during recuperation. Musicians should avoid second jobs that require hand-intensive activities such as computer terminal operation, typing, waiting on tables, etc. As symptoms subside, resume normal daily activities gradually. Meticulous attention to minimizing or eliminating the stress of daily activities on the hands and arms can make the difference between success and failure in the treatment of overuse injuries.

Surgery or cortisone injections are rarely indicated, except for conditions such as carpal tunnel syndrome or certain types of tendinitis (such as at the base of the thumb), which often respond well to injection or surgery if conservative treatment is unsuccessful.

Splinting to rest the injured part is often helpful, particularly when the injury is in the dominant hand. It is very difficult for a right-handed person with tendinitis of the right arm to remember to use the other hand instead. To prevent hand use, the splint should come all the way out to the tip of the finger. Be careful, however, that you don't provoke injury in the opposite arm by the added, unaccustomed use of that side. Take the splint off several times a day to do gentle movements and muscle contractions that prevent stiffness and soreness of the splinted part. For maximum comfort and fit, have splints custom molded by an occupational therapist.

In summary, the overuse injury, which can be the bane of the student or professional musician, can often be prevented or treated successfully in its early stages by increased awareness and recognition of the problem. Prevention, as always, remains the best medicine.

"By overusing the hand, I got into the wrong mode of using my muscles, and now I have to retrain them."

-Peter Oundjian

Surviving Overuse Injuries   13

By Edith Eisler

WHO WOULD THINK that playing a musical instrument could be dangerous to your health? Yet when pursued to excess, even this benign activity has its occupational hazards: witness the alarming number of performing musicians who have become victims of their own success by developing severe symptoms of overuse.

One of these is Peter Oundjian, who had to resign from his fifteen-year leadership of the Tokyo String Quartet in 1996 because of a strained left hand. Since then he has built a flourishing conducting career and recently he was appointed artistic director of the Caramoor Music Festival. However, he is also determined not to give up playing the violin, and is working out a careful regimen of practice to regain the full use of his hand. For the benefit of other players with similar or potential difficulties, Oundjian describes, with generosity and acute insight, his problems, their probable cause, and his current efforts to undo the damage.

Obviously, the only sensible thing to do when a hand gives the first alarm signal of strain is to stop playing, but with commitments planned far in advance, how can a busy performer do that? The situation is infinitely worse for members of a chamber ensemble: roped together like mountaineers–"joined at the hip," as one of the afflicted puts it–they depend on one another for the group's survival. When Oundjian's hand began to show signs of overuse, the Tokyo Quartet was celebrating its twenty-fifth anniversary season with worldwide performances of the complete cycle of Beethoven Quartets, among the most strenuous works in the quartet literature, physically and emotionally. And of course it is the first violinist who is at greatest risk: his part is the most demanding technically, his position as leader the most stressful.

"I knew what was happening," says Oundjian, "because I was losing strength and control of my third and fourth fingers. But I couldn't do anything about it, I couldn't control the situation. I've always played with great intensity, and that probably increased the physical tension as well." And the nervous strain of not being able to trust completely the usually automatic reflexes of his hand in performance must have been enormous. He says he found that he had to practice more than usual, both to feel secure and because he had to re-finger certain passages, which no doubt aggravated the condition further. He also remembers having to use ice often to ease the tension in his hand.

Of course he initially consulted various specialists, none of whom could pinpoint the problem with certainty. Those at the Miller Institute, New York's well-known haven for musicians and dancers with work-related ailments, recommended some physical therapy. One doctor suggested performing an operation on the elbow to relieve possible impingement on the ulnar nerve, which could affect the third and fourth fingers. "But I had nerve conduction tests, which turned out normal, so the uncertainty of the diagnosis did not seem to warrant such radical intervention. An operation is a measure of last resort, and I wasn't ready for that," Oundjian explains. "However, the possibility that I have some nerve damage has not been ruled out, because my third and fourth fingers definitely feel less stable. In order to make them feel stable, I have to completely relax the back of my hand and make sure the first and second fingers are totally relaxed. I don't remember ever having to do that before.

"I finally came to the conclusion that by overusing the hand, I simply got into the wrong mode of using my muscles, and now I have to retrain them. I talked with other instrumentalists who had similar problems and had worked on them on their own, by trial and error and experimentation, looking for different ways to play, different techniques. And I talked at length with a very well-known guitarist who actually managed to rehabilitate his hand and was able to perform again several years later.

"I believe the key problem is teaching the fingers to release. We are very good at putting them down, it's what we do all the time; what we must practice is picking them up again, going back into neutral. Otherwise," he declares, "you're just grinding the gears."

Oundjian often sees and warns against this problem in his teaching. "You know, people are always saying they love to teach because they learn such a lot. You think they are just trying to be nice, but it's true, you do learn a lot, because you have to rethink everything, and you get to see things from another person's point of view." Although he had taught chamber music at Yale with the Tokyo since 1981, he only began teaching violin there in 1995. He now has six students whom he manages to see almost every week. "I dedicate my time to a certain amount of teaching because I love to do it," he says. "It brings me new energy to sit down and try to sort out somebody else's problems. When you spend time with one individual, talking about how to approach the instrument, you really learn all the time. Teaching also ensures that I practice a bit, because sometimes I just have to grab a student's instrument and say, no, let's try producing a sound like this. I don't believe that constant demonstration is the best way to teach, but an occasional demonstration is important.

When I studied with Galamian and later with Dorothy DeLay, both great teachers but basically not players, they used to pick up my fiddle sometimes and say, let me show you how to move the hand, how to hold the wrist, how to move the fingers and release them." As he speaks, Oundjian demonstrates with his left hand, using a finger of the right hand as a substitute fingerboard. "To teach," he continues, "you have to know how a good hand should make a sound, how it should feel, and move, and balance, how weight should be used. Should the third finger come down with the fourth or not? Should the first finger stretch away from the others, should they spread like a flower or come in and support each other? I personally believe in spreading the fingers like a flower as much as possible, especially if you go high up on the fingerboard; I think it gives a good counter-balance and prevents the hand from getting tight. Even in the low positions, I don't believe in holding fingers down very much, unless of course they are going to be used very soon afterwards. I think the muscles should constantly be trained to release; that's a very important part of playing an instrument."

One might think that his students at Yale, who are fine, accomplished players, would have advanced beyond basic problems like these. "No, not necessarily," he says. "Certain problems are never fully resolved. To make a beautiful sound with the fourth finger after an awkward stretch or a shift, for example, might be difficult anyone; even the greatest fiddlers are constantly working on such things. Galamian used to say, we have ten robbers; we have to watch them all the time. And Pinky [Zukerman] always says he practices constantly to keep his technical equipment in order and to rethink what he does, because your hand as well as your energy changes from year to year."

It's difficult to know how much and how soon one should practice after an injury, but Oundjian doesn't think that practicing does his hand any harm. "I feel that the only way I'll ever be able to play with my old freedom is to practice very

HEALTHY STRING PLAYING

consistently and reasonably," he says. "Then perhaps gradually I can retrain my muscles to do this natural release again that we are actually all born with, and that we don't even think about while our hands are healthy and functioning properly. I still haven't really figured out exactly which of my muscles don't release, or which muscles cramp up, because of course it happens unconsciously. So I have to use these techniques of release all the time, quite consciously, or my hand goes into a spasm during which I simply cannot play. By now I have a sense of how to get that release, but I have to concentrate on it constantly when I practice to be able to get the right balance." Clearly, this is a grueling process requiring an extraordinary degree of determination, persistence, and courage.

Generally Oundjian tries to practice at least an hour every day. However, at the Caramoor Festival this past summer, he played in a short piece for four string quartets, and to prepare he practiced as much as two hours a day. The work was written by a nineteenth-century Dutch conductor named Van Bree, "who thought his orchestra needed to learn to listen and play together better, so he wrote them this piece," explains Oundjian. "It's charming, light, a little like a Mendelssohn movement, and a lot of fun, but you have to play together very well to bring it off. So instead of conducting, I played first violin in the fourth quartet. It was the first time I played at Caramoor since I went there with the Tokyo. But it's very hard to hear sixteen people, so sometimes in rehearsal I stood in the middle playing from memory. It shows the importance of a conductor; his hands seem to reflect what you're hearing, and that makes the coordination so much easier! The best way to rehearse this piece would be with a conductor a few times and then just listen, listen."

Oundjian continued to play with the Tokyo Quartet for a long time after his hand problems began, which, naturally, affected the group's ensemble. "It was a strange situation," he reflects. "We were supposed to be on top of the world, but actually we were, or at least I was, swimming for the shore. But we managed; it was a question of survival. We were a very strong team and they were all incredibly sensitive. They helped me by covering for me sometimes. Kikuei [Ikeda, the second violinist], who is a very strong player, had quite a brilliant way of playing just a little bit louder occasionally when he sensed that I was perhaps feeling a little insecure about a passage, or playing a little softer when he could tell that my hand didn't have enough strength and I needed to be a bit more soft-spoken than usual."

He adds, "Of course, on some level I'm disappointed that I couldn't help letting myself be pressured into playing so much that I can't play freely now. But you have to look at the other side: I would never have got to conduct all these wonderful symphonic works if I had stayed with the quartet."

Fortunately, you can do plenty to prevent injury or nip minor problems in the bud.

-Darcy Lewis

Preventing Overuse Injuries: The Power Is in Your Hands

14

By Darcy Lewis

EVEN THE MOST stellar professional athletes know their glory days on the field or court are limited. Their careers are dictated by a combination of talent, hard work, physical skill, healthy habits, and good fortune in avoiding injury.

The same dynamic applies to string players' experiences—with one vital difference. Because music isn't physically demanding in the same way as football or basketball, we imagine we should be able to lead vibrant lives for decades after even the most resilient professional athlete is relegated to watching from the stands. Yet many players are unable to do so, either succumbing outright to overuse injuries or continuing to play in discomfort, hoping the pain will be better tomorrow.

Rich as classical music is, sensitivity to body mechanics or ergonomics (the science of designing and arranging objects for safe and efficient use) isn't one of its strengths. Paganini caprices played by children, marathon practice sessions, even the demands of tyrannical conductors are admired regardless of the physical toll they exact. What's worse, a very real stigma clings to those afflicted with overuse injuries. The recent difficulties of former Tokyo String Quartet violinist Peter Oundjian, who resigned in 1996 because of an intractable hand injury, have at least raised public awareness. However, his misfortune probably exacerbated other suffering musicians' unspoken fears: if him, why not me? They worry not only that an injury can end their careers but that any loss of privacy can lead to lost work. Either way, many musicians who should seek medical assistance don't. Even musicians who have insurance often decline to file medical claims related to repetitive stress injuries for fear of the professional ramifications that may result when they begin to wear some kind of apparatus or don't play for awhile.

Clearly something is awry. Music-making should include joy; at bare minimum, it should cause no pain to any musician, regardless of skill level or professional status. Pain-free playing is most vital to professionals, but it's also important to beginners, because an early understanding of proper body mechanics and good musical habits can prevent debilitating damage later. An increasingly accepted fact of life in American workplaces needs to be embraced by musicians as well: work, specifically work conditions, must fit the worker, not the other way around. Seemingly harmless repetitive movements can eventually damage the body in a complicated chain reaction of hair-trigger physical responses from nerve to muscle to ligament and back again.

Among dozens of specific diagnoses for overuse injuries, focal dystonia and carpal tunnel syndrome are two of the most common. "Repetitive stress injury" and "cumulative trauma disorder" are also correct but vague terms. "They're not a diagnosis as much as an explanation of how the problem developed," says Dr. Heidi Prather, director of the Medical Program for Performing Artists at the Rehabilitation Institute of Chicago (RIC). It's generally no mystery what causes overuse injuries: too much playing or bad physical habits, musical and otherwise, are usually the culprits. "I have literally never worked with a musician whose neck and back weren't factors in their cumulative trauma disorder," says Cara Klausner, an occupational therapist who works with Prather.

"Many patients wonder why I start by working with their necks, but the upper body is often the key to what happens with the hands and wrist."

Prather explains that it's common for tight pectoralis (chest) muscles to pull a musician's shoulders forward, which can then cause neck problems when he or she strains to look up. Also, compressed nerves in the spine or near the collarbone can cause pain or numbness in the hands, says San Francisco hand surgeon Robert Markison. "Musicians will always pay the price for postural mistakes, whether it's immediately or long term," says Markison, himself a wind instrument player who has carpal tunnel syndrome. "When you feel pain, you're doing something wrong and you need to stop."

You should also know that there is some truth to the conventional wisdom that upper-string players are susceptible to left-side injuries, while right-side maladies tend to be the bane of the lower-string players. Dr. Alice Brandfonbrener, founder of RIC's program, is quite vocal about her frustration with violists who insist on playing dangerously large instruments. Markison mentions the danger to people with perpetually cold hands and loose joints. "It's very difficult to heal and maintain hands that are cold. A warm-handed patient will heal twice as fast as a cold-handed one," he says.

Overuse injuries also offer several warning signs. Beware of persistent numbness and tingling in your hands, particularly while you sleep; these sensations may awaken you, or you may notice them as you're waking up, still in bed. Pain or swelling that continues after you've rested and not played for some time needs attention; so does one hand or limb that appears larger than the other. Watch for persistent loss of fine motor control, too: "If doing that smooth, ingrained run of scales now feels either delayed or inadequate, you need to see someone," says Prather.

Fortunately, you can do plenty to prevent injury or nip minor problems in the bud. "As musicians, we're all responsible for maintaining our physical and musical health," says Markison. "Patients who slide into denial about overuse injuries are the hardest to treat. The best patients are those who want to be able to make truth and beauty via music without pain and believe they shouldn't have to suffer."

Look at your personal habits first. Realize that smoking constricts blood vessels, while caffeine and alcohol dehydrate your system. Markison advises keeping these to a minimum, while boosting fluids, especially water, and vegetables in your diet. He also suggests limiting meat because of potentially harmful chemicals used in processing. (Along these lines, avoiding produce grown with the help of pesticides may be a healthy idea, too.) The point here is to remember that what you put in your body does affect your health.

Also, what you do with your body matters. Brandfonbrener is especially concerned about many musicians' habit of "power" weightlifting at the local gym, because of the stress it places on the joints.

Next, consider your playing environment. If you rehearse in a hall that is too cold or too dark, make changes or ask for an improvement. Request a better chair; if you can't get one and your chair is too high, put dark colored books (which will be less conspicuous during a performance) on the floor to use as a footrest. "Maximize your controllable factors by limiting the horrible ergonomic situations in performances when possible. At least get everything right when you practice alone," says Prather, who adds that her patients have gotten away with a surprising number of onstage improvements as long as they were inconspicuous.

Perhaps the most important factor is to plan your musical life and ration your playing time as much as possible. Rise above the minutiae of the day-to-day and look at the big picture of rehearsals and performances over a span of time. That's easier said than done, but the stakes are high. "If you have a recital in April, you should be practicing for it in October, not waiting until March to start," says

Brandfonbrener. "Try to do more no-hands practicing, where you look at the music until you hear it and feel it. Learn new parts over several sessions rather than all at once."

Many musicians think the solution will be a period of rest, whether they dread it as the ultimate loss or rely on it to save them a trip to the doctor. Neither is likely to be the case. "Acute inflammation will usually resolve itself even if the person doesn't rest, but that leads to chronic pain without inflammation and microscopic muscle tears," says Prather. "That's why, even though rest is important, it won't solve problems alone." After a brief rest period, Prather generally has her patients increase their playing time by ten to twenty percent each week, keeping an eye out for complications and gradually increasing the time as their health improves.

When you need help, it's best to find a professional caregiver who understands both upper-body anatomy and music. If you don't know of such an expert, start with your usual doctor if you feel comfortable with his or her responses about your problem. Or contact your local university medical school or visit the Performing Arts Medical Association's website to find a member. Also, find out whether your state allows a one-time evaluation (future visits require a physician's prescription) by a physical therapist. And keep alternative methods in mind; acupuncture, in particular, has been effective for carpal tunnel syndrome. No matter whom you see, be sure to take your instrument along so you can demonstrate exactly what you're doing when you feel discomfort.

"You're entitled to ask a tremendous amount from a potential treater because you ask so much from yourself and, in turn, the world asks so much from you as a musician," says Markison. "Physically, the musicians I see have very typical occupational overuse injuries, but they tend to follow everything I say, probably because they have so much at stake and are already so disciplined," says Klausner. "I typically see patients for only a few sessions, so it's key that the patient is an active, self-guided, independent partner in their healing process."

A large part of that process, experts agree, is to adopt a regimen of warm-ups. Most overuse injuries are resolved by appropriate exercises and correct posture, the cornerstones of any healing program. (In fact, says Markison, only ten to twenty percent of his patients require surgery.) "Every musician, injured or not, should do appropriate upper-body warm-up exercises before playing," Klausner says. Markison notes that a growing number of exercise videos are available, including *Therapeutic Exercises for Musicians*.

Physical therapy and regular exercises have made a difference for violist Don Ehrlich. "Physical therapy may be our salvation as musicians, especially when we bring the right attitude to our healing process," he says. Ehrlich, assistant principal violist of the San Francisco Symphony, has suffered three playing-related injuries over the past nine years and is a perfect example of how rest and exercise can heal and maintain health. "With my first injury, I thought my career was over, but healing exercises and resting brought me back to my viola in a month," he says. Ehrlich then began a warm-up exercise routine and, even though he later injured himself again, believes that the routine allowed him to play his 17-inch instrument as long as he did. "Before I started the exercises, it used to take me 20 to 30 minutes of playing to feel warmed up. But with them, I can now walk out onstage and be playing full tilt in five minutes." Fortunately, Ehrlich's musical health, not to mention his peace of mind, has been restored without him suffering permanent damage.

What we can all learn from Ehrlich's experiences, and those of countless others, is that attaining and keeping musculoskeletal health is the key to how long and how well we're able to make music. We can't change human anatomy and we can't play without making repetitive movements; we must learn to reconcile the two. The sooner the musical community acknowledges the pain and fear of injury that often go along with string playing, the sooner the many already injured musicians can get help and heal without professional repercussions. As we become more open about our occupational hazards, the students who follow us will learn that the potential for their musical health lies within their own hands, and that making great art doesn't have to, and shouldn't, hurt.

Warm Up Before You Play

"A runner would never run a marathon without stretching, but what most musicians do every day is the equivalent," says Dr. Heidi Prather, director of the Medical Program for Performing Artists at the Rehabilitation Institute of Chicago. Prather suggests this exercise regimen as a general guideline for warming up healthy muscles before playing, but check with your own physician or a licensed, registered occupational or physical therapist before beginning any exercise program.

The routine begins with the large muscle groups and works toward the small ones. Stand while doing each move; perform each smoothly and with moderate speed, avoiding jerky or rough motions. Do between five and ten repetitions of each exercise, but stop if you feel tired and reduce repetitions until you no longer become fatigued.

1. Raise both arms straight overhead above ears as if reaching for something, then relax to sides.

2. Swing both arms outward and upward overhead, then relax to sides.

3. Shrug shoulders by bringing them up as close to ears as possible, then relax.

4, Hold arms at shoulder height, parallel to the floor, with elbows folded like chicken wings. Then press shoulder blades backward to "meet" in center.

5. Do forward shoulder circles. Arms should hang at sides. Repeat, reversing direction.

6. With elbows against your sides, open and close both elbow joints fully as if bringing two hand weights simultaneously to your shoulders. However, this move is not like a bicep curl; instead, the tips of your thumbs (not the insides of your wrists) should point toward the floor, then toward the ceiling.

7. Hold forearms out straight, elbows against your sides. Hands, wrists, and forearms should be in a straight line. Smoothly flip wrists over so that palms alternately face the ceiling, then the floor.

8. Holding forearms parallel to the floor and hands in loose fists, flex wrists up toward the ceiling, then down toward the floor, keep elbows against your side.

9. Hold hands flat out in front of you, palms down, rotate wrists away from center toward the little fingers, then back toward the thumbs.

10. Hold forearms out in front of you, palms down. Spread fingers wide as possible, then gently squeeze them together. Keep hands flat.

11. Hold hands flat out in front of you, palms down. Curl the outer two knuckles of each finger in toward the palm, keeping the innermost knuckle as still and straight as possible. The shape should resemble a hook or claw more than a fist.

Often poor playing posture is the result of poorly adjusted [chin and shoulder] supports.

-Avram Lavinsky

Double Trouble   15

QUICK ACTION CAN HELP ADDRESS POTENTIALLY DEBILITATING DOUBLE-CRUSH INJURIES

By Avram Lavinsky

A DOUBLE-CRUSH INJURY can sideline a string player, but learning about the cause, prevention, and treatment of this malady can increase your chance of avoiding a serious problem, or recognizing it in time to seek professional medical help. So what is a double-crush injury?

There are a number of tight spaces in the upper body where nerves supplying the arms and hands can become entrapped, but three are particularly common sites of injury among musicians. Pressure from the collarbone, the uppermost rib, or the slender muscles that attach nearby can injure a major network of nerves resulting in a condition called thoracic outlet syndrome. Very common among violinists and violists is damage to the ulnar nerve (ulnar neuropathy) as it rounds the inside of the elbow at the area commonly known as the funny bone; this entrapment is known as cubital tunnel syndrome. Among musicians and nonmusicians alike, the most common sight of injury to the median nerve is the dreaded carpal tunnel of the wrist.

Frequently an individual shows signs of injury to the same nerve at two such locations.

Since the early 1970s some researchers have advocated a theory that once a nerve is injured higher in the body, it may be more susceptible to a second injury nearer to the hand and fingers, a condition termed double crush.

Dr. Michael Charness, founder of the Performing Arts Clinic at Brigham and Women's Hospital in Boston and professor of neurology at Harvard University, remains ambivalent about the cause and effect nature of double crush. "Do I see patients who have thoracic outlet syndrome and cubical tunnel syndrome? I see a lot of them," he says. "I'm just not sure that one of them has caused the other. They're both so common in my practice that when they occur together, it doesn't necessarily make me want to conclude that the thoracic outlet syndrome caused the ulnar neuropathy or contributed to it."

Theory aside, Charness emphasizes that all nerve entrapments require medical attention early on. "The very early phase of these is the phase at which it's easy to avoid long-term problems," he says. "It's better to get on top of these things before a person actually does develop weakness."

| Good | Fair | Bad | Very Bad |

Early Intervention

Regina Campbell, founder and director of Performing Arts Physical Therapy in Brookline, Massachusetts, has been working with musicians for over two decades. She, too, stresses the importance of early medical intervention. "For the ulnar neuropathy, if they get help in the initial stages when they first notice numbness and tingling, the problem can usually be fixed by resting for a period of time, wearing elbow extension splints at night, and gradually resuming playing, and then after that maintaining good practice habits," she says. "If you don't address it right away and the ulnar neuropathy continues over a long period of time, that's when the patients need surgery."

Campbell acknowledges that choosing the right doctor or therapist can be difficult. "The patients should definitely play their instrument for the [healthcare] provider, and that's why it's really important that whoever they're going to knows something about treating musicians and what the proper postures are for playing the instrument."

Charness agrees. "There are lots of good doctors who know how to take care of nerve entrapments," he says. "There aren't as many who are sensitive to the specific occupational issues [relating to musicians]. If there is somebody who's experienced in performing arts medicine then it's probably preferable. I think it's essential, in some respects, to watch a musician with their instrument. The problem is that not everyone knows what to look for."

Problems brought on by specific playing postures are often missed by sophisticated nerve studies and imaging techniques done in a more relaxed position. "I have people play, and then I re-examine their hand strength after I hear them play," Charness adds. "That type of exam is, in my experience, more helpful, more predictive of the outcome, and more useful in guiding my treatment than any radiographic test."

Problematic Posture

Faulty posture can cause multiple nerve entrapments. Allowing the shoulders to round forward for marathon practice sessions can lead to thoracic outlet syndrome, but it also has the mechanical side effect of increasing the bend at the elbow for violists and violinists, and this in turn can cause cubital tunnel syndrome. Often the solution is to hold the instrument more to the side, maintaining a more relaxed position for the left shoulder blade, keeping it further back.

Charness points out that keeping a relatively straight, relaxed wrist is the key to avoiding carpal tunnel syndrome. "Carpal tunnel can be a technical challenge," he explains. "If a person is maintaining an odd angle in their hand while they play, no amount of therapy is going to help them; they have to have a more neutral wrist where it's possible."

Often poor playing posture is the result of poorly adjusted supports. Chin rests and shoulder rests that are not high enough force elevation of the shoulder, increased tension for the neck muscles, and thus increased thoracic outlet syndrome.

For cellists, an endpin adjusted to an excessive length can have a similar effect. Charness also observes the height of the instrument's bridge. "I see people who are having problems with carpal tunnel syndrome or hand pain whose bridges are too high, whose strings have to be pressed too hard to make contact with the fingerboard. So I do look at some technical issues because sometimes fixing them is more important than anything else we do."

Elbow Flexion

Posture and equipment are not the only issues. "Regardless of the person's posture, prolonged elbow flexion is one of the occupational risks of playing the viola or the violin," Campbell says. "It's more their playing habits: how long they're playing without taking a break."

Charness concurs. "We see people who are playing two or three hours at a time without taking a break, or playing eight hours a day. Those are the ones who are getting in the most trouble."

For players who have to use every minute of practice time, Charness advises recording the last five minutes of each twenty-five minute practice session and then spending another five minutes listening to the tape. Most injuries surface after a sudden increase in playing time or intensity, so it's crucial to ramp up slowly for recording sessions, auditions, major performances, and the return to music after a layoff. Duress to the upper body due to day jobs and hobbies should be weighed against practice time as well.

Campbell emphasizes regular exercise to speed the healing process and decrease the risk of injury. "I think it's really important," she says. "I think walking is great. Musicians might not have the time to go to a gym and work out, or they're traveling, on tour, things like that."

But time spent exercising can pay dividends. Decreased muscle tension can improve the quality of sound that the patient gets out of the instrument and it can also build endurance, Campbell says.

The medical and musical worlds are becoming increasingly aware of the stresses to health faced by musicians.

-Shannon Mar

Stress and the String Player   16

By Shannon Mar

Personal Preparation Log

JANUARY 15: During student/faculty conferences today, I decided to enter the Leipzig Competition on July 12. My professor says I need two major concertos to be fully qualified, plus the Paganini Caprice No. 24 and a Beethoven violin sonata. Wow, that's a lot of work. But I'm up to the challenge. I know I can do it well...

January 30: Finished getting all the music this past week. Practiced six hours today. Do I have to keep up this pace for all of the next six months? Yes, I know I can do it.

February 20: Practice going well, but performance weak so far. Mock performance shows some stage fright that needs correction. Social life really suffering; my friends and family do not understand why I'm putting in so much work.

April 20: Practice not going well right now. How can Olympians do this every day for so many years?

May 20: Practice much better. All I can think about is music. How will the Russian judges like my playing? Do we still have Cold War bad relations? Having a lot of trouble sleeping lately—had a bad cold the last couple of days. Wasted the beautiful weekend getting over it.

June 20: Lots of trouble sleeping. Constant music review during all my waking hours. (Then it's all over in less than five minutes? Is this what life is all about? A few minutes of glory?) Final mock performance went very well. Concert hall full of sound. This is going to go great! Some visa trouble today, but should be resolved before I leave.

June 28: Left yesterday, arrived today. Wow, what a greeting at the airport! We all feel so welcome and important! Felt bad, though, when I snapped at the bellboy for dropping my luggage at the hotel. I should not let this pressure get to me.

July 3: First round went great! I can hardly wait for the results! Why do they take so long? Gee, the waiting is nerve-racking. I can't decide what's worse: the stage fright before performances, or the waiting.

July 8: During practice today, I yelled at my accompanist for her slow tempos. I quickly apologized for my behavior. She smiled and said she understood what I was going through. Haven't been able to sleep too well lately—again.

July 12: Still alive—can't believe it! Played the Paganini Concerto in the practice session with the conductor today. I hope I didn't use up all my good performances before the real thing. He was rather difficult to get along with, however.

July 14: Over at last—and I got second place. Not bad! The level of playing was very high. I talked to some future concert promoters today and exchanged business cards. What a blur; this week went by so fast! I need to sleep, I'm so tired. And my forehead feels kind of hot.

Every string instrument player can identify with this fictional account of a violin competition participant. Players at every level experience some aspect of the stresses of competition, whether they're beginners in the Suzuki method, students auditioning for their chair in the school orchestra, or the most famous soloists preparing for a concert. Daily practice, new music to memorize, exercises to learn, rehearsals, auditions, competitions—all these make up the lives of many a string player.

I play the violin, and I remember the stress and anxiety of recitals and playing before people who were judging my performance. This was long before performance psychology, prescription drug use, and plant extracts were commonly used by performers. I thought that perhaps my professional studies in drug development might be put to good use in trying to understand the causes of stress, its physiology, and some prospective solutions.

When performance becomes everything, a level of stress arises that puts musicians at far higher risk for stress-induced illnesses and syndromes than most other professions, according to David Sternbach, a social worker in Silver Spring, Maryland who researched the issue in the March 1993 *Maryland Medical Journal*. Three major factors are involved. The first is stage fright, arising form public performances. (In a 1986 survey published in *Senza Sordino*, the publication of the International Conference of Symphony and Opera Musicians, or ICSOM, this was the number one cause of stress cited by orchestral musicians.) Second, the scrutiny of conductors at rehearsals and performances makes players feel they are the subject of constant criticism. Finally, perfection (note-perfect performance) is expected all the time, with no second chances allowed. Audiences are conditioned by recordings to expect such performances, and musicians are acutely aware of these unrealistic standards.

The medical and musical worlds are becoming increasingly aware of the stresses to health faced by musicians. Charles O. Brantigan, M.D., a cardiovascular surgeon in Denver, stated his view most poignantly at a symposium on the medical problems of musicians, held at the Aspen Music School in 1985. "It's worth backing up and looking at the roots of stage fright," he said. "I'm not a musical educator, but I train surgeons and occasionally perform. I see a big difference between the musicians I perform with and the surgeons

I teach. With our surgeons, we try to create an expectation of success. Most of the musicians with whom I am associated have an expectation that there is going to be a problem. I think this is largely a result of their training, which tends to make them anxious and produce stage fright." Even Dorothy DeLay admits that teachers and performers contribute to the problem, "I remember being backstage before a concert with Piatigorsky and a student of his," she said at the same symposium. [Piatigorsky] came into the room and said, 'Dear, how do you feel?' She said, 'Fine.' He said, 'I don't want you to be nervous.' She got a little more tense. This went on for ten minutes. Finally he said, 'I'm going to listen in the back, I'm sure you're going to be all right.' By the time he finished she was shaking!"

Just how does your body respond to stress? A stress stimulus causes a fight-or-flight response and the release of corticosteroids, hormones from the adrenal gland. Increased hormone levels cause the physical symptoms of stage fright: increased blood pressure and heart rate, rapid breathing, dry mouth, upset stomach, and often tremors in the hands and knees.

Knowing this, what should you do—simply suffer through these challenges, considering them intrinsic to the string player's lifestyle? Or can you do anything positive? String musicians have successfully used psychological counseling, aerobic exercise, hypnosis, yoga, the Alexander Technique, massage therapy, and many more methods to combat stress.

In spite of the increasing interest in mind and body techniques for improving practice and learning to relax, the *Senza Sordino* survey of musicians found that prescribed medication was the method tried most often (by forty percent of the respondents) and most often considered successful (by ninety-two percent). When treating stage fright, beta-blockers are the most widely known and prescribed. Propranolol, which goes by the trade name Inderal, competes for receptor sites with stress hormones, blocking their effect. Beta-blockers are normally used to treat high blood pressure, heart conditions, and migraines. These drugs block the effects of performance anxiety: rapid heartbeat, hyperventilation, increased blood pressure, dry mouth, shaking hands, and wobbly knees. Although the drugs do not stop the underlying anxiety itself, the theory holds that, by blocking these undesirable effects of stage fright, a musician can improve musical performance. According to Dr. Alice Brandfonbrener, the director of the Medical Program for Performing Artists at Northwestern Memorial Hospital in Chicago and another participant in the Aspen symposium, beta-blockers are well-tolerated and have a good safety record when properly used, especially for short-term or occasional use for performance anxiety in normal people.

What are the drawbacks to using these drugs? First of all, they are not specifically approved by the FDA for treating stage fright, but only for high blood pressure, heart problems, migraines, and similar conditions. Most medical professionals recommend the drugs for temporary alleviation of stage fright symptoms that can jeopardize a performing career, but they say beta-blockers should eventually be replaced by non-drug therapies to avoid psychological addiction. Secondly, the side effects can be major. People using these drugs have been known to report sleep disturbances, hallucinations, depression, fatigue, and cold hands and feet. In addition, these drugs should not be taken by diabetics or people with asthma or heart failure. Finally, some users have reported unpleasant physical sensations and a kind of detached feeling.

It makes sense that drugs that suppress unwanted physical signals may block desirable ones as well, thus interfering with a performer's physical response to his or her music. With such major drawbacks, musicians should not share or borrow these drugs from friends or family, as is commonly done with drugs of this popularity and wide use. *Above all else, these drugs should only be used under medical supervision.*

One major problem not addressed by beta-blockers is the issue of stress-related illness. Increased stress hormone levels can lead to suppression of the immune system and an increase in illness. For any professional, the very conditions so common for musicians—shift work, workplace location changes, and constant economic insecurity—chronically exacerbate stress levels and susceptibility to colds, flu, and other illnesses. And downtime due to illness is detrimental to musicians' schedules, performance quality, psychological health, and income, especially during the winter, when illnesses abound. Ninety percent of all U.S. citizens come down with at least one cold during an average year (the total cost in medical bills and lost work days is about $2.5 billion per year), according to a 1994 report in *The International Journal of Sports Medicine*. But highly-stressed people had double the incidence of upper-respiratory tract infections over a six-month time frame, compared to minimally-stressed individuals. And because many microorganisms are now resistant to most commonly used antibiotics, many people have less success using them to try to recover from infections.

Some people are now starting to hear about an alternative to beta-blockers, nontoxic plant substances known as adaptogens. Considered safe by the FDA, they put people into a state of increased resistance to stress, making them better able to resist illness and adapt to extraordinary challenges. Several plants are classified as adaptogens, including *Eleutherococcus senticous (E.S.)*, *Schizandra chinensis*, *Aralia mandshurica*, *Rhodiola rosea*, and *Rhaponticum carthamoides*. First tried medically in the Soviet Union during the 1950s, these plant substances were used with great success in international athletic competitions and the Russian space program. The most famous, most often used, and best-studied adaptogen is the thorny bush known as E.S., from the Middle Amur region of Russia. Not to be confused with Chinese gingseng, this plant was discovered by I.I. Brekhman in the

1950s. After testing it among athletes, Professor A.V. Korobkhov concluded that it could increase stamina and endurance and improve reflexes, reaction times, and concentration. The substance accelerated the restorative processes after intensive activity.

Research done in 1987 in the former West Germany proved the power of E.S. to stimulate the immune system in a clinical trial. The extract increased all immune cell counts by as much as eighty percent in healthy volunteers, with no side effects seen up to five months after administration ended. Work like this is so promising that clinical trials in AIDS and cancer patients are currently in progress here in the U.S. As for downsides, the most persistent problem now noted is uneven extract quality and, if taken on an empty stomach, fatigue (observed in some athletes).

Taking substances, be they synthetic drugs or plant extracts, is not for everyone. The most important thing for the stressed musician to understand are the causes and symptoms (physical and mental) of anxiety, and the dangers of using any prescription drug without medical supervision. Then you can begin to research your own best method for reducing stress. One thing that is clear is that a healthy immune system, which is promoted by lowered stress responses, helps prevent infections; promotes more consistent, high-quality practice and rehearsal; and lowers the risk of missed competitions, recitals, and concerts.

Knowing these facts, musicians can look into the many options available for controlling performance anxiety. No longer should stress dominate and control the life of the string player.

Might it be possible not only to defeat the fight-or-flight response, but also to set yourself up for a better-than-normal performance?

-Gabriel Sakakeeny

From Fear to Freedom   17

DEVELOPING A NONDRUG STRATEGY FOR COMBATING PERFORMANCE ANXIETY

By Gabriel Sakakeeny

IT'S DARK BACKSTAGE. Everything's ready. I'm ready. I *am* ready. Just wish that damned conductor would stop talking and get on with it...Oh! It's Jerry. "Hey man, good to see you." Break a leg. Jeez. What if I break a string? Just need some water. Stage manager looking at me. Probably thinks I'm nervous. I *am* nervous. Shoulders feel tight, chest tight, have to take a deep breath. I haven't been breathing. Must be nervous. Fingers are cold and damp. Feeling a little dizzy. Why didn't I pick something easy to do, like brain surgery? I'm okay, I'm fine.

Sound familiar? Anyone who performs has experienced these thoughts and feelings at some time or other. Some people experience a mildly heightened tension that can actually enhance performance. At the other extreme, even seasoned performers can be almost completely incapacitated by nausea, memory loss, shakiness, dry mouth, intensely loud inner dialogue, and loss of connection with time and reality in general. No matter how well you've prepared your performance, the grip of fear can cost artistic expression as well as negatively affect your career, your reputation, and your self-esteem. It's worth looking not only at the underlying causes of performance anxiety, and the most common drug therapies, but also at an alternative approach to dealing with it. This way you can get on with doing what you love best, unencumbered by fear.

The Mechanics of Fear

In some circumstances, the mechanism that gives us performance anxiety can be very beneficial. Normally, our autonomic nervous system operates in parasympathetic dominant mode, letting us cruise through life blissfully ignorant of the majority of our body functions. But when you perceive a danger, like a car unexpectedly swerving into your lane on the freeway, your sympathetic nervous system kicks in to protect you. It injects your bloodstream with a hormone called epinephrine, also known as adrenaline, which increases your heart rate, heightening your alertness and reaction time, and constricting the blood flow in your arms and legs so that blood is concentrated in your torso. This all happens in milliseconds, instantly setting you up to deal with the emergency. Known as the "fight-or-flight" response, this mechanism evolved to protect us from predators in the primeval jungle.

The problem with this response is that its effects are exactly the opposite of what you need to give a good musical performance. If you play an instrument, you want your blood in your finger muscles, don't you? And how about those shakes? Having your muscles jacked up is great for running away from tigers but not so great for playing with a bow. The effects of triggering this mechanism also last for much longer than the immediate need to run away or battle with a predator. When it comes down to it, fight-or-flight is good for just that and not much else. It's about survival.

Bypassing the System

Some people who are strongly affected by performance anxiety have turned to suppressing the symptoms chemically. The intention is to mask the symptoms or to block the epinephrine receptors of the sympathetic nervous system, thus neutralizing the effects of performance anxiety. The strategies range from very mild approaches, like eating a lot of bananas, to such serious means as alcohol consumption or using prescription drugs called beta-blockers.

Drinking alcohol or using illicit drugs before performing might depress your nervous symptoms, but it can have a negative effect by slowing down your reaction time and distorting your sensory perceptions. Substance abuse can become addictive and have a negative impact on the health of your heart, liver, and other internal organs.

Using beta-blockers like propranolol, also known commercially as Inderal, will block the effects of epinephrine in key parts of the body. It can also cause uncomfortable side effects depending on how much you take and your body's reaction to it. It will not make you play better, nor will it "cure" your problem. It will relieve only the physical manifestations—rapid heart rate, shortness of breath, sweating—resulting from the fight-or-flight response. While some musicians swear by Inderal, others say that while leaving them free to execute technical challenges, the drug makes it difficult to express the emotional and musical aspects of the performance. It apparently has little or no effect on dry mouth, and can cause such adverse conditions as tingling or numbness in the extremities. Get a doctor's opinion and supervision before trying this approach.

The bottom line on chemically bypassing the sympathetic nervous system is that you may get up to your normal level of playing at best, possibly with some unwanted side effects. This might be a big relief for those who are powerfully affected by performance anxiety, but perhaps there are other ways to control the problem. Might it be possible not only to defeat the fight-or-flight response, but also to set yourself up for a better-than-normal performance? Let's take a look at a subtle approach to dealing with performance anxiety, examining the problem in a new light. Remember that fight-or-flight is supposed to be a response to a perceived threat to our survival. But giving a concert, taking a lesson, or even playing an audition isn't life threatening, really. What is it that is being threatened so much that our sympathetic nervous system takes over, puts us on automatic pilot, and gives us the butterflies? It's certainly not our physical hardware. Maybe it has to do with our software.

Parasitic Memory Activation

There is a mental phenomenon, which I call parasitic memory activation (PMA), that seems to be part of every human being's design. Here's an example: You're driving down the freeway listening to the radio and all is well. The tune changes to a piece that you're working up for an audition in two weeks. In an instant, you have that sunken feeling in the pit of your stomach, your breath gets tight, and you find yourself obsessing about your instrument, practicing, and whether or not you should go into law instead. It's as though something has invaded your mind and is using it without your control. What's happening here? What's the mechanism?

If you think about it, your past exists as a set of memories, some conscious, most not. Certain events get burned into memory more deeply than others. Do you remember what you had for breakfast three days ago? Probably not. Do you remember the name of your first sweetheart? Probably. Why? Because the things that stick are either very pleasant or very painful. Remembering pleasure gives us good feelings. Remembering painful failures and threats calls up fear, embarrassment, sadness, and anger.

Now consider this: You and I have probably accumulated thousands of failures, threats to our self-esteem, insults, and slights to our ego over years of performing and being trained in music. There's a wide and deep pool of negative memories around music for us to draw upon. Every time we encounter something in the present that looks even vaguely like a negative experience in the past, we experience a flood of emotions, thoughts, and sensations that bring the effect of that memory into the active present. These trigger events can be as small as missing a note unrepentently, hearing a melody, hearing someone's name mentioned, anything that attaches to a past negative memory. Yet the emotional punch of the experience sometimes is many times more intense than the original trigger would warrant.

The automatic response to a perceived threat that musicians call performance anxiety is a musically based PMA. The bad news is that this software mechanism is not going away. We will always be triggered by events in the present that look like painful experiences in the past. And the older we get, the more past we'll have! It's part of the design. So how do we deal with it?

Treat the Cause

When you're in a PMA state, this is what to do. This method has worked for thousands of people over the years and can be mastered by practically anyone.

First, recognize that you've been hijacked by a PMA. Being aware of this mechanism can help you put your emotions in perspective. Next, discern what triggered the PMA. Triggers usually are events that happen in the present that resemble negative experience in the past or that somehow are "wrong" from our current point of view. Finally, notice that you are adding drama to the event. The feelings and sensations you have during a PMA are just noise automatically generated by your software. Just observe them like noticing the weather. Experience them as something you have, not something you are. For example, "I have some nausea," not "I am nauseated."

Performing these three steps usually will decrease the intensity and duration of the PMA. With practice, you will have regained your composure before anyone notices you are in a tizzy. There is another possibility that can alter your whole relationship to playing and to performance anxiety.

Invent a New Game

In the competitive world of music, you're only as good as others say you are, or at least that's how you may interpret the situation. We're brought up to meet the standards of our teachers, conductors, contractors, and other players. Because so much of our sense of self is tied up with how we play, and that measurement is always subjective and decided by others, we are very much victims of other people's opinions. This is a hell of a way to live your life.

What if you invented a new reason to play music? Not to make money, or to be well thought of, or to achieve some adolescent fantasy of fame. What if music were about serving something bigger than yourself? For instance, if your purpose in playing were to attain an aesthetic ideal of beauty, then your major concern would be giving yourself and the audience an arresting experience of timeless wonder and awe. Your preparation and performance would be organized around providing that and any thought of yourself would be completely missing. It's not about you; ergo, no survival threat and no performance anxiety.

Changing the game is an effective strategy. Many people over the years have placed themselves in service to community, to God, to beauty, to the development of children, and so on. As a result, they've found that their performances excelled beyond any level they could predict. There are even orchestras in which this game is practiced. Whatever possibility you choose to follow, if you allow yourself to be inspired in that service, you will be free of any limitation that your machinery imposes. Be inspired!

This work gives people choices in how they will use their bodies.

-Jon Bernie

A Different Kind of Practice

18

MUSICIANS AND THE ALEXANDER TECHNIQUE, A CONVERSATION BETWEEN JORJA FLEEZANIS AND JON BERNIE

By Jorja Fleezanis and Jon Bernie

FLEEZANIS: Although as students we may be under a lot of pressure, the magnitude of tension in the life of a professional musician is beyond what most students can imagine. Large concert halls require a large sound, and many musicians struggle to produce that sound. The demands of rehearsals and performance schedules put pressure on our limited resources, and that pressure builds and manifests in bodies which are in pain, in muscles which are working hard but ineffectively. Tension becomes entrenched as it accumulates. Would you concur with that?

BERNIE: I certainly would. People get so oriented toward performance in playing the instrument that the experience of the body as the primary instrument is lost. The Alexander Technique is about integrating body and mind. That means learning to become conscious of the body in such a way that the head, torso, and legs are activated when playing an instrument.

FLEEZANIS: How do you actually go about this?

BERNIE: Different teachers have different approaches, but there are basic areas that most certified teachers cover. Learning to identify areas of tension involves movement work—from simple movements such as walking, sitting in a chair, and standing, to more complex activities such as bending over, reaching, lifting, sitting at a computer terminal, playing an instrument, any activity in which we use our bodies. In working with someone, the teacher will put his hands very gently on the head-neck region, training the person to become sensitive to that area so that it is free and light and energized. Alexander lessons also generally involve therapeutic table work where people wear comfortable clothing. It is very gentle, hands-on work—moving legs, moving arms, moving head and neck, training people to become conscious of certain holding patterns in their bodies, so that they can release them, and so that they can learn to release them on their own. Initially, it may be easier for a person to become aware of a problem when they're on the table than when they're moving.

Jorja Fleezanis and Jon Bernie

FLEEZANIS: One thing I learned right away is to be conscious of the head and its relationship to the spine. If we abuse this relationship, we really undermine our energy.

BERNIE: That relationship is the essence of the work. What motivated you to start taking Alexander lessons, and what has motivated you to continue?

FLEEZANIS: A colleague of mine at the symphony told me about the Alexander Technique. She said it was the newest thing—this was some years ago—to help musicians and address their particular kinds of strains, and that she was going to a teacher. I noticed in the course of rehearsals that she was transforming, changing. She looked like someone who had added something new to her presence on the stage. I can only describe it as a sort of vitality that was coming from her, energy that I had not been aware of before. She also seemed to be using her body in a more complete way. I didn't only focus on her arms as she played the violin; I was aware of her whole body.

BERNIE: How did the Technique first affect you?

FLEEZANIS: In the first six or seven lessons I learned to think about things I had never thought about, physical habits I had developed over the years.

BERNIE: You started having a new experience with your body. You started to become conscious of the habits that were causing problems.

FLEEZANIS: Yes, and it was a real conflict. I didn't want to give up those habits.

BERNIE: People often stop their Alexander lessons at that point, when faced with that conflict.

FLEEZANIS: I had that very reaction, except that I was definitely in pain, continually finding that the pain had to do with stress and not knowing how to defend myself from it. So I kept going to the lessons. It was a massive undertaking, but the effects were dramatic. I was learning an extremely hard piece for me—the Brahms Double Concerto—and I made a breakthrough while I was studying it. I relearned how to play the instrument through studying the Technique. There were things I had always been convinced I was unable to do. I assumed that my practice methods were not at fault, but that some things were just beyond me. And then as I learned to integrate the physical freedom and muscular flexibility from the Alexander Technique with information I already had about how to play the violin, a potential in me started coming out—like talent that had been held back. I learned to set priorities under pressure. I found that when I was playing a difficult passage, I might not be thinking about the music, but about my body. For instance, my left shoulder, which may have been pressed or contracted or distorted, might have been preventing me from doing something technically. I learned to ask myself: Is my shoulder allowing me to vibrate the way I want, or to reach that tenth? As I learned to train myself without forcing myself, to become, in essence, my own biofeedback machine, these adjustments allowed my ease to be greater, and that encouraged me, because I was sounding better with less effort. Eventually I began doing things I had no idea I could do.

BERNIE: What kind of pain were you experiencing when you first began Alexander lessons?

FLEEZANIS: When I first came to the Technique I had muscle strain and pain in my calves and thighs, and I think it was because I would lock myself in my chair. The chair became a kind of post I would cling to when I got into danger, and all my muscles felt they had to wrap around it like a snake—even if I was just leaning my foot against the chair. Somehow my muscles were like tentacles grabbing onto the chair so that my fear, my stress and insecurity were manifesting as counterproductive muscle tension.

BERNIE: This is an example of how we use a lot more effort than we need to when playing an instrument. People can get stuck. We hold on. Learning the Technique is about learning how to use your muscles efficiently, and not waste energy. It's not just relaxation. It's learning to expand on each movement rather than contract. What you get is a greater flexibility using your muscles, so that you do not compound a tense moment by holding on to it for the next forty minutes.

Alexander was an actor who developed a serious problem. He would lose his voice during performances. Doctors were unable to help him. Through years of self-observation and discovery he developed his Technique. Alexander actually discovered some basic physiological laws of movement and how human beings function optimally. He was able to retrain himself, to prevent habits of misuse and to avoid pulling his head back and down on his spine. His technique isn't so much about learning good posture per se, but about learning how to have a relationship of head to torso and legs, where the moving parts are dynamically alive and in relationship to each other.

FLEEZANIS: All of this suggests that musicians, who either sit or stand while they're working, freeze their muscles because their bodies are used to just standing still. What can eventually result is a weakening of some muscles and an overuse of others. I was sabotaging energy needed by my arm by tensing my leg.

BERNIE: That's right. When I go to the symphony I watch the musicians and conductor. How are they distributing their effort? Some of the musicians remind me of that wonderful line in *Ulysses*: "Mr. Duffy lived a short distance from his body."

FLEEZANIS: How does an Alexander practitioner work to help people live in their bodies?

BERNIE: An Alexander teacher basically functions as a coach. We are therapists in some sense, but we are also teachers and give people tools that they can use to help them recover their birthright of poise.

FLEEZANIS: Meaning?

BERNIE: Meaning that we had it, and we can regain it. What we learn in this technique is not a set of exercises. We don't plaster over old habits with new habits. This is an uncovering of our natural flexibility, our natural poise.

FLEEZANIS: I see that kind of flexibility in my cat. Does that make sense?

BERNIE: Sure. Watch how a cat moves. It uses its whole body. There's fluidity to it. We really can regain that kind of fluidity. It's almost as if everything becomes a kind of dance involving the whole body.

FLEEZANIS: What should motivate one to start using the Technique?

BERNIE: Pain motivates a lot of people. But the work is primarily preventative. It's re-education. We can learn how to prevent problems before they occur. It's an investment in the future.

FLEEZANIS: Can you describe a typical Alexander program?

BERNIE: A good rule of thumb for people who are starting out is a lesson once a week. Sometimes people want more frequent lessons. If they can afford that and they have the time, that may be preferable. Generally speaking, a session lasts an hour, though it can be as short as half an hour. The price ranges from $25 to $50 per lesson. Between 10 and 30 lessons are necessary to give people a handle on what the work is about. After that, they can continue to take lessons weekly or monthly. Group lessons are more economical, and you get the chance to see other people being worked on. I think the limitation of group teaching is that you get very little time with your teacher actually putting his hands on you. It's easy to get the wrong idea about what the work is because you are not getting enough feedback from the teacher.

The Technique is not about fixing. It is about developing a dynamic, conscious, passionate relationship with one's self. This work gives people choices in how they will use their bodies. It's not that we will never again misuse our bodies— of course we will. But we become more sensitive to how we distribute our effort.

To understand why yoga is so helpful, it is important to understand why a seemingly innocuous endeavor like playing an instrument is potentially so dangerous.

-Lauryn Shapter

Injury Prevention and Healing Through Yoga   19

By Lauryn Shapter

AT THE ONE HUNDRETH anniversary celebration of the Berlin Philharmonic, the late Yehudi Menuhin conducted the opening of Beethoven's Fifth Symphony. What was unusual about it was that Menuhin conducted with his feet while standing on his head, a trick he learned from many years of practicing the ancient art of yoga.

A dedicated student of the Indian yoga master B.K.S. Iyengar, Menuhin was keenly aware of the benefits of yoga, particularly for musicians. He was introduced to Iyengar in the early 1950s when, during a concert tour of India, he developed severe muscular pain. Menuhin became a regular practitioner of the art, inviting Iyengar to travel throughout Europe in 1954 for his first yoga demonstrations in Switzerland and France.

My own discovery of the benefits of yoga for string players came quite by accident, almost ten years after I had left graduate studies in violin performance at the Manhattan School of Music because of a severe and persistent case of tendinitis in my left wrist. I had sought the advice of various medical professionals, from hand surgeons to neurosurgeons to physical and sports therapists to acupuncturists. I had explored myriad ways to play, altering my left-hand position, adjusting my playing posture, and trying new chin and shoulder rests. After eight years and only minuscule progress, I became convinced there was nothing I could do to play without pain. I decided to leave the profession altogether.

Unfortunately, mine is not a unique story. Career-ending injuries are all too common, particularly among string players. Although it is certainly not the only path to prevention and healing, the benefits of regular yoga practice now seem all too obvious to me—yet it is an option of which many musicians are unaware.

In the forward to Iyengar's *Light on Yoga*, Menuhin writes that yoga is "a technique ideally suited to prevent physical and mental illness and to protect the body generally." This "ideal technique" not only serves to prevent physical illness, particularly the kinds of problems brought on by playing a musical instrument, but also assists in the healing of overuse injuries.

To understand why yoga is so helpful, it is important to understand why a seemingly innocuous endeavor like playing an instrument is potentially so dangerous. Regardless of the type of instrument played, the muscular and skeletal systems are considerably compromised for long periods of time. Elevating the arms not only causes contraction in the muscles, but also interferes with healthy blood circulation. The manner in which the violin and viola are held puts a significant strain on the neck, and the twisting action of the left arm further constricts blood flow.

Not only is the body in general compromised, but musicians tend to use their bodies asymmetrically. This is most noticeable with the violin and viola, but is evident with the cello and bass as well. In addition, certain areas of the body (the arms and hands, for example) are given a rigorous workout during playing, while other parts remain relatively dormant. Sitting or standing for extended rehearsals or practice sessions, without the benefit of significant lower-body movement, further increases general stiffness.

Because of the wrist's easy flexibility and mobility, compounded with the hand positions string players use, injury often occurs there. But the locus of pain may not be where its root cause lies; often, the difficulty in finding this root cause makes it harder to zero in on a cure.

So much for the bad news—news with which most musicians are already quite familiar. The good news is that yoga offers a counter effect. Although there are eight "limbs," or branches, to the art of yoga (such as meditation and breathing techniques), the focus here will be on the third limb, the *asanas* (physical postures) of yoga.

Over the years, the practice of yoga has earned a well-deserved reputation as an antidote to stress, primarily due to its focus on conscious breathing and relaxation. Many people, however, are unaware of the deeper physical benefits of this ancient art. Because yoga is a whole-body system, the *asanas* exercise virtually every part of the body and intentionally incorporate the mind and spirit as well, making it a system unlike most exercise programs.

Dr. Gail Dubinsky, a physician and yoga instructor in Santa Rosa, California, specializes in soft-tissue orthopedics (the kind of repetitive-stress injuries common to musicians, such as carpal tunnel syndrome and tendinitis). She uses yoga extensively in her practice and has developed a program called "RSI? Rx: Yoga." As Dubinsky explains, "Yoga works on posture and balancing the tension in the upper body. The standing poses ground you and take away excess energy blocked in the upper body."

Musicians often react with great skepticism (and sometimes disdain) when I speak about the role yoga has played in my recovery. Unfortunately, many believe that yoga requires tremendous flexibility and the willingness to twist oneself into pretzel-like positions while chanting something unintelligible. Contrary to popular opinion, the art of yoga (if not every pose in yoga) can be practiced by people of any age or fitness level.

"People ask me what poses are good for carpal tunnel syndrome, what are good for tendinitis," says Dubinsky. "With a few exceptions, all the poses are good. A lot of people have a limited range of motion, so sometimes adaptations are necessary."

One of the most basic and fundamental *asanas* in yoga is *Tadasana*, or Mountain pose. A seemingly simple pose, *Tadasana* works on standing posture, teaching the practitioner to balance body weight evenly from the front to the back of the foot, as well as how to center the weight evenly between both feet, rather than leaning on one or the other. It also teaches proper alignment of the spine and pelvis, which with regular practice creates a postural awareness that translates to everything you do, from washing dishes to playing your instrument. Improved posture allows the skeletal system to do its job of supporting the body, preventing the back muscles from straining to maintain proper posture. I have found that improved posture has been paramount in helping me work through long practice sessions without excessive muscle fatigue.

Practitioner Tracye Lederer demonstrates the basic Mountain pose (left). The Downward-Facing Dog (below right) and Upward-Facing Dog (below left) are especially good for string players.

Standing poses are the foundation of any yoga practice. Poses such as *Uttihita Trikonasana* (Triangle pose), *Uttihita Parsvakonasana* (Extended Side-Angle pose), and the three *Virabhadrasana* (Warrior) poses all contribute significantly to strengthening and stretching the lower body. Taking care of the lower limbs helps maintain healthy circulation; the benefits continue even while the legs are relatively inactive.

Strengthening and stretching poses include Warrior pose I, Warrior pose II, Triangle pose, Extended Side-Angle pose, and Warrior pose III.

These poses also offer tremendous benefits to the upper body. The first two Warrior poses and the Triangle pose create an openness and expansiveness in the chest; relief for stiffness in the shoulders, neck, and back is immediate. The Extended Side-Angle pose lengthens the spine in an intense stretch that extends from floor to fingertips. According to Patricia Walden, director of the B.K.S. Iyengar Center of Greater Boston, if you can find time to do only one pose, it should be *Aldo Mukha Svanasana*, or Downward-Facing Dog, as it gives many of the benefits of the other poses. This pose resembles a dog when it is in play stance, its front legs extended forward and back legs straight. When doing this pose, the hips are raised and the body creates an inverted V, with the torso and arms in line. The fingers are stretched wide open and placed flat on the floor, creating a much-needed counter effect to the left hand finger action used while playing. Downward-Facing Dog is also excellent for relieving stiffness in the shoulder-blade region; it is a pose I use frequently during breaks in rehearsals or when I have just finished practicing.

The opposite pose, *Urdhva Mukha Svanasana* (Upward-Facing Dog), is a mild backbend in which the spine arches backward and the face points upward. Like all backbends, it opens the chest, strengthens the spine, and relieves back strain. It also counteracts the effects of long practice sessions, by stretching the arms, legs, back, and neck.

Yogic breathing techniques are also considerably helpful in the healing of injuries, although they are not typically taught to beginners. "Abdominal breathing evokes the relaxation response, which promotes oxygenation and healthy blood flow," says Dubinsky. "Better blood flow improves healing."

There are literally hundreds of *asanas* in existence. In general, they can be divided into several basic categories: standing poses, forward bends, backbends, inverted poses, and arm balances. Each group of poses can benefit string players and, used together, they offer a total body workout. Standing poses are, again, the foundation of a yoga practice. Forward bends help lengthen the spine and stretch the legs, while backbends counteract the effects of poor posture and hunching. Inverted poses help improve circulation and give relief to the legs after long periods of standing, and arm balances are superb for upper body conditioning.

Besides the more obvious physical benefits, yoga has a subtle advantage over many other forms of exercise. Its union (yoga means "union") of the mental, spiritual, and physical helps people manage stress, improve concentration, and create balance. Musicians—with unorthodox working hours, hectic schedules, and the mental and physical demands of performance—can become victims not only of playing-related injuries but also of stress-related diseases. In relieving immediate and accumulated stress, yoga reigns supreme.

Any musician struggling with a playing-related injury should seek medical help. But a musician often needs to assume responsibility for his or her own healing. The real beauty of yoga is its ability to help prevent injury in the first place, by offering counter movements that relieve current physical strain and years of accumulated repetitive motions.

I am not an advanced practitioner of yoga, nor am I a doctor or a physical therapist. I am a musician who finally found a way to play without pain, through my own internal investigation of how my body works, my own exploration into listening to the wisdom of my body. I tried yoga out of curiosity, without the slightest inkling that it would be the path that returned me to music. But the more I practiced yoga, the easier my playing became, until one day I realized how long it had been since I had suffered that crippling pain in my wrist. And nearly ten years to the day after I came to the conclusion that I would never again play without pain, I made the decision to allow music again to be the primary focus of my life. Yoga gave me a way back to my very first love: playing the violin.

Getting Started with Yoga

There is a plethora of yoga styles available to those interested in developing a practice. B.K.S. Iyengar, Yehudi Menuhin's teacher, has developed a precise and safe method of learning yoga that uses props (such as blankets, blocks, and straps) to help beginners learn the poses. The ideal way to learn yoga is with the assistance of a certified teacher. As with any learning situation, different people are comfortable with different teaching styles. Trust your gut instincts when choosing a teacher. In most metropolitan areas there are many teachers to choose from; even in remote areas, the number of yoga teachers is growing steadily.

If classes are not given locally, if your schedule makes it difficult to attend classes, or if you simply prefer the privacy of your own home, there are a number of videotapes and books available. Below is a partial list of resources. Remember, though, that executing the poses correctly is critical; it is best to take a weekly class.

How to Use Yoga by Mira Mehta (Rodmell Press). Extremely user-friendly step-by-step guide to 41 poses chosen especially for beginners. Outlines a ten-week course and includes a section on *asanas* for common problems.

Light on Yoga by B.K.S. Iyengar (Schocken Books). First published in 1966, *Light on Yoga* is considered by many to be the bible of modern yoga. Extremely detailed descriptions and photos, but may be overwhelming to beginners.

A Matter of Health: Integration of Yoga and Western Medicine for Prevention and Cure by Dr. Krishna Raman (Eastwest Books). This is an excellent and thorough reference book for anyone interested in the therapeutic benefits of yoga. Although not easy to obtain because it is not published in this country, it is well worth seeking.

R.S.I.? Rx: Yoga! by Dr. Gail Dubinsky. This video is a guide to healing carpal tunnel syndrome and other overuse injuries of the hands, arms, and upper body. Dubinsky specializes in soft-tissue orthopedic injuries and is a yoga teacher as well.

Yoga Journal's Yoga Practice for Beginners, with Patricia Walden. This videotape and written practice guide provide a clear, concise introduction to yoga. Poses are explained in detail and repeated several times for thorough understanding.

Yoga Journal's Yoga Practice for Strength, with Rodney Yee; *Yoga Journal's Yoga Practice for Flexibility*, with Patricia Walden. These videotapes build on *Yoga Practice for Beginners*, and are excellent for advancing your practice.

The fabulous thing about Pilates is that it doesn't just align you.

-Felicity Vincent

Pilates for the Cellist 20

By Felicity Vincent

CELLO WIZARDRY EXPLODED in the twentieth century. During its last decades in particular, better teaching, better communication, and easier access to recording raised the general playing standard out of all recognition. In such an increasingly competitive atmosphere, every ambitious cellist strives to work through the repertoire, achieve technical prowess, and add to the c.v. as quickly as possible in order to satisfy teachers and the world "before it's too late." But it's never too late. Cello playing at a high level is a whole-life issue and musical expression involves the entire emotional spectrum, which increases over the years.

Performance calls for intensity and an adrenaline-charged energy. It calls for stamina and the self-knowledge demanded in creating and releasing muscular tension. It calls, in short, for whole-body awareness.

Because cellists constantly use the left and right sides so differently, muscular development is asymmetrical. You might argue that a cellist needs different strengths on each side. But muscular systems function best in balance; balanced muscular recruitment ensures a minimum of wear and tear on joints. Over the years, muscular imbalance can begin to pull bone structures out of kilter, as unstretched muscles tighten, coordination suffers, and pain sometimes results.

Alexander teachers have been realigning musicians for decades. Yoga, Qi Gong, and Feldenkrais all teach breath control, balance, the ability to let go of tension, and postural and general self-awareness. But Pilates seems to answer cellists' specific needs best of all. It is the exercise system for performers—dynamic, demanding, extremely organized, and, in the studio, painstakingly well taught. It doesn't set out to affect your mind, it's a system dancers and athletes have used for almost three quarters of a century, both to help recover from injury and to enhance performance. Sportsmen now train regularly in a variety of areas to promote overall muscular fitness. Why not learn like them to put stress on your body in a controlled way, so that you'll be able to lead a physically and musically full life into old age?

After studies in London and three years in the Halle Orchestra, I had the great good fortune to come under Janos Starker's critical eye. He showed me a "whole" view of cello playing, and I began to be aware of body use. But I found it difficult to let go of habitual muscular patterning and work from my supposedly strong back muscles, and I didn't understand fully the importance of what he was teaching me.

Some years later I acquired a glorious instrument totally unsuited to my build. I couldn't move while playing it; even worse, it didn't allow me the pelvic stability (that is, the possibility of sitting firmly on both sitting bones) necessary to promote my full power. Muscular imbalance led to weakness in my right arm, which in turn led me to a Pilates Body Control Studio. There I immediately felt at home.

Often it is muscular imbalance leading to tightness that causes pain. And once you feel discomfort you become afraid to exercise. Pilates training enables you to isolate muscle groups and exercise "around" an injury. The body is realigned, and the knowledge gained from recognizing your supporting (stabilizing) and mobilizing muscles, plus the empowering effect of thoracic breathing, give you a new basis from which to develop the way to play consistently at your best. Nor does it matter what your build is. I'm a five-foot, slight, pliable specimen of *Homo Cellisticus*. Pilates has made me much stronger and helps prevent damage to my ligaments. Big and heavy cellists, on the other hand, can be helped to increase their mobility.

Pilates teachers know about bodies. Often ex-dancers, they know how to use their own, and have had to learn anatomy and kinesiology as well as the Pilates method. The training is *serious*! When, at the beginning of your first session, you stand with your back to your teacher and roll down to the floor, he or she will recognize your tight and weak places, and, if you're in pain, quite possibly see where it is stemming from.

The author demonstrates an exercise on a Pilates Plié machine.

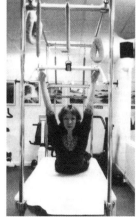

This Pilates machine is called the Cadillac.

There are two essentials to Pilates: pelvic stability and thoracic breathing. In the studio you will first learn extremely minimalist-seeming movements designed to mobilize your lower spine and pelvic area. Tight hamstrings often contribute to lower-back discomfort, so you will gently stretch them. Then you will set about creating your Pilates core (also known as your powerhouse) by working your abdominal muscles, which will help support your lumbar spine and maintain your pelvic placement.

Muscles basically fall into two groups: stabilizers and mobilizers. The stabilizers, which are strong and able to support heavy movements, include the abdominals, the long back muscles or *latissimus dorsi* (beloved of Janos Starker), and the buttocks. (In such a brief study it isn't possible to mention all the layers of complementary muscles.) The mobilizers aren't designed to take strain. If forced to, they become over-strengthened and tight. Take, for example, the muscle in the top of the shoulder, the upper trapezius. It is all too easy to play an instrument using this muscle far too much. And tightness here triggers the highest proportion of cellists' problems. The neck loses its flexibility and the shoulder joints their mobility, forcing hyperextension of elbows and wrists. And hyperextension is something to be avoided at all costs— next stop, tendinitis!

It is vital to use your stabilizing muscles optimally and to keep your spine mobile. In Pilates you learn the control needed to articulate your vertebrae, supporting the movement with your abdominal muscles. In the studio you also work with resistance devices (springs and light weights) or simply against gravity to become aware of, lengthen, and strengthen the muscles down your sides and in your back. Your body begins to understand that these somehow connect with the muscles of your pelvic floor. Now your Pilates powerhouse is taking shape; you are developing an indestructible trunk and supporting the branches, which are your arms.

Pelvic stability is hard for cellists to achieve. Is there a cellist alive who doesn't turn predominantly to the left? You necessarily support the cello with your left leg while the right is free to relax—outwards or inwards, whichever is more comfortable. Either way, the hip flexor comes under strain and there's a temptation to sink into the right side. In order to engage full power from a sitting position, it is necessary to have both sitting bones evenly and firmly placed on your chair; and having both feet weighted equally firmly on the floor will provide the pelvis with yet more stability.

Thoracic breathing is crucial to Pilates. You learn to soften the ribcage down and breathe in deeply across the back, and perform strong muscular movements on the exhale. This is the area that has most changed my platform confidence: my ribcage has expanded and, with it, the strength between my shoulder blades. I've done neck stretches, and I have discovered the amazing mobility that is possible in the shoulders when they are not slumping forwards. It's as if the playing power transfers directly from a strong Pilates center to the arms, sparing my shoulders and neck, and with the breath I really feel I am "singing" the cello.

The fabulous thing about Pilates is that it doesn't just align you. Joseph Pilates was, among other things, an acrobat. From the stability of your strong center, you are able to discover an increased supported range of mobility. Cellists in particular need this; they must be able to cover the length of their strings with the left hand and the length of the bow over the positions that are imposed by four strings. So how do you revolve between the A and C strings? Keeping pelvic support and sitting up out of the hips, you can achieve a good deal of rotation with a slight turn of the body above the waist. You can learn the movement properly in the studio. And, remember to perform it twice as many times to the right!

Intense abdominal support and work on the full range of your back muscles will also take you into thumb position without raising your shoulders. You may need to come onto your toes and curve your upper body slightly, but we're all different, so experiment. Again with firm support from the abdominal muscles, you will learn how to extend the spine backwards, opening out the chest—exhilarating! And there are also stretches for the arms and wrists, which should never be neglected. Aerobic work, such as walking or swimming, is also very important.

The system is best learned in a well-equipped studio under the super-critical eye of a trained teacher. You are challenged to learn new movements and to work ever deeper, in order to achieve your full potential, your full *playing* potential. Pilates helps you recognize your own personal needs. It has improved my concentration, and led me to the instrument that's right for me and the voice that is mine. It helps me serve music as best I can.

About the Contributors

Jon Bernie is a violinist and a full-time Alexander Technique practitioner based in San Francisco. Along with public teaching and leading retreats, Jon has had a full-time private practice in San Francisco for the past 22 years. Certified in Zero Balancing , Alexander Technique, NLP, and Amanae, as well as trained in Self Acceptance Training, Ericksonian Hypnosis, Cranial Sacral Therapy, and eye movement emotional release work, Jon integrates emotional and hands-on therapy from the perspective of deep interconnected beingness. Visit www.zerobalancing.com.

Carrie Booher is a 2004 Master of Occupational Therapy graduate. Her musical background has included study at the Peabody Institute's preparatory division, and she continues to play as a chamber musician. She plans to specialize in the prevention of work-related musculoskeletal disorders in musicians.

Ruth F. Brin has published books of poetry and nonfiction, including *Harvest*, and a memoir detailing life in the Twin Cities during the Depression era. She also served as a book reviewer for the *Minneapolis StarTribune*.

Yvonne Caruthers is a cellist in the National Symphony Orchestra of Washington, D.C. (since 1978). A graduate of the Eastman School of Music, she played with the orchestras of Syracuse, Rochester, Denver, and Buffalo before taking her position in Washington. Ms. Caruthers has appeared as concerto soloist with the National Symphony Orchestra, the George Mason University Symphony, and the American Youth Symphonic Orchestra. She gave the Washington, D.C. premiere of Leonardo Ballada's *Concerto for cello and nine wind instruments*. She also teaches privately.

Edith Eisler, *Strings* magazine's corresponding editor in New York, is a violinist, violist, and teacher who has written for the publication since its inception in 1986. She began studying the violin at the age of six in her native Vienna and has performed solo and chamber music in Europe and North America. "Having been on the other side of the footlights most of my life gives me a certain perspective in interviewing musicians and writing concert reviews," she says of her regular contributions to *Strings*. She is also a contributor to *Stagebill*, *Chamber Music*, and the CD-reviews sections of Amazon.com and *epulse*.

Jorja Fleezanis has been concertmaster of the Minnesota Orchestra since September 1989, assuming that position after nine years with the San Francisco Symphony, eight of them as associate concertmaster. She has played numerous concerts in the San Francisco Bay area and the Twin Cities with the FOG Trio, which she founded in 1984 together with pianist Garrick Ohlsson and Michael Grebanier, principal cellist of the San Francisco Symphony. Ms. Fleezanis is also a member of the faculty at the University of Minnesota, where she teaches violin, conducts courses in orchestral and concertmaster training, and leads sectional rehearsals.

Joan Hamilton has been a Biotech reporter for *Business Week* since 1983, and bureau chief from 1986-87. In 1985, she left the magazine briefly to help launch the BioWorld information service. Author of numerous cover stories on biotechnology and health, she is also a contributor to *BioPeople* magazine, *The Stanford Magazine*, and *Stanford Medicine*.

Tom Heimberg is a violist in the San Francisco Opera Orchestra and a former member of the San Francisco Symphony. He has also served as orchestra manager for the Opera. His music studies included two years in Paris as a

Fulbright Scholar and Teaching Fellow, and he later did studies in the psychology of practice. For more than two decades he has taught the Art of Practice as an extension class at the San Francisco Conservatory of Music. He's currently on the board of directors of the San Francisco Performing Arts Library and Museum, and Local 6 of the American Federation of Musicians.

Joanne Horner (Chapter 4, "It's a Stretch")

Janet Horvath is associate principal cello with the Minnesota Orchestra. A recent recipient of the Richard J. Lederman Lecture Award presented by the Performing Arts Medicine Association, she founded the "Playing (less) Hurt" Conference series. She performs as a recitalist and soloist and lectures on injury prevention for musicians and is also a nationally recognized authority and pioneer in the area of medical problems of performing artists. She has also published articles in professional journals, spoken at conferences, and presented master classes on the topic.

John Jerome has written two books on the physiology of athletics, *The Sweet Spot in Time* and *Staying With It.*

Avram Lavinsky (Chapter 15, "Double Trouble")

Darcy Lewis is a violist and award-winning freelance writer in Riverside, Illinois. Her work has appeared in the *Chicago Tribune*.

Julie Lyonn Lieberman is an improvising violinist, singer, composer, educator, recording artist, author, and producer. Formerly on faculty at Juilliard, New York University, and The New School University's Jazz Program, she now teaches privately in her NYC studio. Lieberman is the author of seven books, instructional videos, and has written over 55 articles for string- and music-related publications.

Shannon Mar is a violinist, a drug-development researcher, and the author of several articles on adaptogens.

Derek Noll (Chapter 4, "It's a Stretch")

Richard Norris, M.D., directed the Performing Arts Medicine Clinic at Braintree Hospital in Braintree, Massachusetts. He was also on the faculty of the New England Conservatory, where he taught a course in Health Education for Musicians.

James Reel is a freelance writer and editor covering the arts, literature, and border issues for the *National Catholic Reporter*, the *All Music Guide*, and *newmusicbox*. Formerly, he was the editor of the *Tucson Weekly* and classical music critic and arts/entertainment editor at the *Arizona Daily Star*. Reel is a contributing editor for *Strings*, and has recently taken up the cello.

Gabriel Sakakeeny, video communications manager for Agilent Technologies, earned a bachelor's degree at the San Francisco Conservatory of Music in 1985 and a master's in orchestral conducting from Rice University two years later. An active participant in the music community of Houston before heading to California, Sakakeeny served as principal conductor of Campanile Orchestra and music director of the Houston Youth Symphonies and Ballet Opera. He also has conducted the Colorado Philharmonic, the Auburn Symphony, the San Francisco Youth Symphony, the San Francisco Waltzing Society Orchestra, the Opus One Ensemble, and the Houston Composers' Alliance.